D1436295

INSIDE THE C.I.D.

INSIDE THE C.I.D.

by

Ex-Chief Superintendent
PETER BEVERIDGE

EVANS BROTHERS LIMITED
LONDON

First published 1957

MADE AND PRINTED IN GREAT BRITAIN BY
THE GARDEN CITY PRESS LIMITED
LETCHWORTH, HERTFORDSHIRE
Z. 5118

CONTENTS

Chapter		Page
One	THE MACHINE	9
Two	THE APPRENTICE	13
Three	PLAIN CLOTHES	28
Four	SOHO AND MAYFAIR	43
Five	DEATH IN DOVER STREET	57
Six	TEA FOR FOUR	72
Seven	THE BARNSLEY MURDER	93
Eight	THE FLYING SQUAD	99
Nine	MURDER TRAILS	125
Ten	DEATH ON THE BEAT	140
Eleven	THE MAN FROM BAGHDAD	153
Twelve	MURDER IN SUBURBIA	162
Thirteen	DEATH FOR CHRISTMAS	179
	POSTSCRIPT	186
	APPENDIX	194
	GLOSSARY	199

ILLUSTRATIONS

Ex-Chief Superintendent Peter Beveridge *frontispiece*

The author's father *facing page* 48

P.C. Beveridge 48

The author as a Seaforth Highlander 48

Plain-clothes Detective Beveridge 48

The Photographic Branch in action 49

Taking a close-up of an automatic pistol 64

Examining clothing for dust 64

Learning to be a Detective 65

Chief Superintendent Beveridge arrests Mrs. Florence
Ransom 96

A group picture taken at the retirement of Sir Norman
Kendal 97

P.C. Nathaniel Edgar, shot dead on duty 112

Superintendent Beveridge leaves the house outside
which P.C. Edgar was murdered 112

Sidney Tiffin, wildfowler, who found the torso of
Stanley Setty 113

Facsimile of list written by Brian Hume 113

Patient paper work helped Superintendent Beveridge
in the Setty case 113

Donald Davidson whom the police sought for questioning *facing page* 160

Agnes Walsh's snake-shaped bracelet and watch 160

Lightning cartoonist Harry Michaelson 161

The author relaxes with his wife and daughter 161

The War that Never Ends 176

A Police Inspection in Hyde Park in 1935 177

The " Big Four " as they were in 1954 177

For permission to reproduce copyright photographs the Author and Publishers are indebted to: Associated Press, Commissioner of Police of the Metropolis, New Scotland Yard, "Daily Mail," " Daily Mirror," "Daily Express," " Illustrated," Keystone Press, Mobile Press Photos, " News of the World," " Star," Topical Press.

CHAPTER ONE

THE MACHINE

WHEN THE TELEPHONE rang just after 10 p.m. I was not surprised. I was pretty sure it was not some friend inquiring after my health and tolerably certain that a big case had opened. I was sitting at home in front of the fire wearing an easy jacket and bedroom slippers, reading a newspaper report on the chances of Arsenal the following day. It was a bitterly cold night in February and I had been looking forward to a quiet weekend.

As I went to the telephone I heard my wife putting on the kettle. She had no illusions about night calls; she had heard too many before.

I picked up the phone and heard the urgent voice I expected. It could have been any one of five divisional detective inspectors. I listened: " That you, guv'nor? " I knew then it was Tom Stinton, in charge of the Southgate area, a young, good-looking and capable fellow. He heard my grunt of acknowledgment and went on: " I've got a murder out here. One of our fellows—shot three times." He gave me a few more essential details and I satisfied myself that the hunt for the murderer was properly started.

I walked back to the sitting-room, laced up my shoes and straightened my collar and tie. Then Margaret, my wife, brought in a cup of tea.

" What's happened, Peter? "

" There's a murder at Southgate. It's one of our own chaps, a fellow called Edgar. He's been shot, going after a burglar," I said.

My wife knew the routine; she had experienced it so many times. It was not a time for asking questions or for showing disappointment that another evening had been ruined. She knew that, as soon as my car arrived, I would be gone, perhaps for several days. While I drank my tea she brought my heavy coat, a thick scarf and my gloves. Then I heard the car draw up and my driver, Jim Scobbie, at the door saying " Hallo " to my wife. I kissed her goodbye and the powerful, radio-equipped car slid off, the tyres crackling on the frosty macadam.

Nine miles away, Police Constable Nathaniel Edgar lay shot dead by the man he had challenged as a suspect. I was about [to take part in another man-hunt, and this time a very personal one. No policeman likes to have one of his colleagues murdered.

I was wide-awake now. The drowsing effects of the comfortable fire and the peace of my home had gone. Now I was only conscious of the car sliding through the traffic under the skilful, trained hands of Scobbie. I did not think of it then, but here I was, the product of one of the greatest crime-fighting forces ever known, and I was in that car, going to yet another murder, because I had been trained by men who had created the Force.

I knew, before that night was out, that every man on duty, and those on duty the following day, would be helping to track down a cold-blooded murderer. The main burden would be on the Criminal Investigation Department, those 1,400 men scattered throughout the 735 square miles of London, the men who work to no time-table. And I knew it would be fairly certain that the Criminal Record Office would take part in the hunt. They are the men who catch criminals on paper, the back-room detectives who keep records of the men and women in Britain who commit any crime from simple theft to murder. In their department are hundreds of thousands of files giving details of convicts and their associates, and some particulars of a private nature which would startle many a criminal if he had the opportunity of reading them.

From the different directions of London I knew that one of the Yard's photographers would quickly be on his way, with one or two of the Fingerprint Department's experts, to see what they could find. The Fingerprint Branch works closely with C.R.O. and the experts sent on murder jobs can read fingerprints with amazing accuracy, tell how they were made, their classification, sex, and often the occupation of the person who left them. Over the years those detectives have caught thousands of criminals who thought they were safe because they were not spotted at the scene of the crime.

Many a time I have sat in C.R.O. and listened to the men there talking to a detective outside who was seeking their aid. He would say: " Anything on Joe Smith, aged about forty-five, from Poplar? "

" What's his second name? "

" Aloysius."

" Anything else? "

" Bit of a stoop on the left side and a quiet talking voice."

" O.K. Hang on."

With that apparently sketchy information the C.R.O. man can work. In minutes he checks the names, then cross-checks with the " Peculiarities " file under " Stoop, left side." In less than three minutes he has a file out.

" This looks like the man you want. He's got some ' form ' for screwing (house-breaking)."

" That sounds like him. Will you send it out to me? "

It may be that the detective outside had a tip from one of his informants, the men known as " stool-pigeons " or " snouts," who are invaluable to detectives. They are not nice people; indeed, most of them have been to prison, but they get results by gaining the confidence of criminals.

They will pass on their knowledge to a policeman they trust, or for a cash payment. And, sometimes, they can be dangerous, setting a trap to get a detective into trouble.

I knew that already a message would have been passed through Scotland Yard's Information Room to all the radio cars, " Q " cars and Flying Squad cars prowling all over London. I noticed a police-box, its light flashing. That would probably be a message about this murder for the man on the beat.

And then there are the uniform men, patiently plodding around, protecting the lives and property of the citizens of London, preventing crime and arresting criminals in between seeing children across the road, catching mad dogs and attending to accidents.

That was how I began, more than thirty years ago—on the beat. And because of that beginning I was speeding towards a murder which experience and training might help me to solve. It all began, oddly enough, when I was walking through London, wearing the kilt of the Seaforth Highlanders, in the year of 1918.

CHAPTER TWO

THE APPRENTICE

ON A SUNNY day in June, 1899, the police constable at Largo, Fife, on the east coast of Scotland, announced what was, to him at least, an item of great local interest. That was my father celebrating my arrival about 400 miles away from London, a place which he had never visited. I grew up, with my two sisters and my brother, in an atmosphere of police stations, police work and hearing crime discussed. One of my grandfathers was a constable and I had two uncles in Scottish police forces.

When I was seven years old, my father was given charge of the County Prison at Dunfermline which in those days, was run by the police. My brother and sisters and I were delighted with this move, for it gave us the opportunity of saying to astonished strangers: " I must go now and get back to prison." On reflection, I suppose the inmates were quite pleased to be there, for it was a pleasant building which accommodated only six men and two women for sentences of up to fourteen days.

My mother looked after the two women, although she had no title. She was the policeman's wife and automatically became part of his job. My father had no assistance in running the prison and we were allowed to play in the two-acres garden where the prisoners worked, kept from freedom by a high wall. To my as yet untutored eye they seemed pleasant enough, always willing to play a game when my father wasn't looking and ever ready to repair my football or mend a puncture in my bicycle.

My passion was then, and still is, association football.

I played at school, dreamed of playing for Scotland and once had an ecstatic two weeks in the prison being taught by a professional footballer who was serving a short sentence for being drunk and disorderly. Just before I left school, when I was fourteen years old, my brother, seven years my senior, joined the Fife police. I became apprenticed to a firm of linen manufacturers. At that time I had already a vague feeling that I would become a policeman but I was still fond of the country and wanted to stay with my friends.

I might never have followed the family tradition but for the 1914–18 war. It had started soon after I left school and every young man in the area was joining up at the earliest moment. Even then I was a fairly hefty lad and, just before my eighteenth birthday, managed to enlist in the Seaforth Highlanders, the famous kilted regiment, and after training at Cromarty was drafted to France. I knew we had to go through London and I was excited to see the great city which to us, in the wilds of Scotland, seemed enormous and far away. But I did not realise how that day was to change my life.

We arrived at Euston and marched through the streets to Victoria. It was the policemen directing the traffic who caught my eye. They seemed majestic and almost god-like in their command of the busy streets with the scurrying people and the traffic, and the background of tall, important looking buildings. As I marched, carrying my pack and rifle, my mind was made up. If I survive, I thought, then London is the place for me.

Fortunately for me there was little of the war left. I was involved in some battles, wounded, not seriously, and demobilised in January, 1919. On the way back another sight of the traffic policemen reaffirmed my decision and I went home and at once applied. While I waited I went back to a clerical job, but my heart was no longer in ledgers.

I did not have to wait long. In a few months I travelled down to London, passed the very strict medical test and a Civil Service written examination, and I was accepted. I went back to my job, and the kindly old boss made an effort to change my mind. " You have a great future here, son," he said. " You're very young and London is a long way from home." I did not tell him, but there was nothing at that time that would have made me change my mind. I packed my bags and went to London to join the training school in the Strand which was called Eagle Hut.

We looked a queer bunch when the class assembled. There were other Scotsmen, Welshmen, Irishmen and quite a few Cockneys. It seemed that we had only about two things in common, the determination to become a police-man and a slight background of war service. If anyone thought this was going to be an easy job, he was quickly disabused of the idea in the welcoming speech. A superin-tendent with smartly curled moustaches who looked as strong as an ox spoke to us with thumbs tucked into the breast pockets of his tunic.

" You will stay here for eight weeks," he said, " and those of you who are any good will be allowed to go on the street, still under instruction. And then you will know practically nothing." He paused, letting his sharp eyes rove over the sea of pink and somewhat startled faces. " This is a tough job and one day you will be on your own in one of these streets, and, for policemen, those streets can be very lonely places. You will make lots of mistakes, you will be disliked by a minority of the people, but they are the ones who will give you trouble. Those who like you won't be so difficult. We shall teach you how to give first aid, how to defend yourself and how to shoot a pistol. And we'll teach you a lot of laws which you must know. One last thing. You have joined the finest police force in the world—don't let it down."

A sergeant bawled us to " Attention " and the superintendent thumped out.

Although most of us had done plenty of marching in the Army, we had to learn all over again. We had to wear stiff collars and walk in a relaxed way at two and a half miles an hour. I realised then why it is that policemen never appear to hurry.

We were taught a form of judo by police champions, how to take a gun from a man, and how to take him to the station if he was truculent. A crack shot taught us how to handle the pistols that are issued to police in times of emergency. It was explained that the London police have never been armed but that there are pistols and ammunition at every station which can be drawn if necessary.

The first-aid classes were intensive. We were taught how to rescue a drowning man, or pull someone from an electric rail, how to apply a tourniquet and stop bleeding, how to diagnose injuries and illnesses.

I thought at first that traffic control would be the most satisfying part of the training but, alas, found it dull. I argued that it was perhaps that we were not doing the real thing—just using other students as vehicles. In fact, much later, I found the real thing just as tedious and quite exhausting.

Best of all was the instruction on the criminal side of police work. Detectives came to the school, men whose names were household words like the famous Fred Wensley, Superintendent Carlin and Jim Berrett, the bearded detective who looked like Hercule Poirot. From them we heard about the craft of identifying criminals, how to look at them and register their features. They gave us basic rules and little memory aids like: " Go from the top; hair, eyes, nose, mouth, age and build." Then they told us to look at the teeth, hands and clothes.

I learned a little about fingerprints, the difference between whorls, arches and loops. It was impressed upon me that I must never disturb the scene of a crime or touch anything. There was instruction on what to do at a fire, or a flood, how to deal with a dangerous structure or a hole in the road, how to summon motorists and keep the streets clear of what are now called " Teddy boys," and how to deal with street bookmakers. It was on this last subject that we first heard about corruption. The sergeant instructor, a well-tried and rather crusty character, said: " The bookies make ready money and they will smell you a mile off. If you get near enough to pinch 'em they will offer you money. Don't take it. Pinch 'em."

The talks on discipline were impressive—and frightening. We learned not to talk to each other on duty—the crime of " gossiping "; not to talk to young women, particularly nursemaids; not to be found absent off the beat; not to smoke or drink on duty. We were warned that we would be severely punished if caught. We had some practice with the truncheon, a fifteen-inch length of hard wood known as " Mr. Wood," and were told never to aim at a person's head but to go for his shoulders or arms. We were also told to keep a tight hold on it, for many a policeman has been hit with his own truncheon.

There seemed to be almost nothing with which we did not have to deal. Sudden cases of childbirth were touched upon; reporting unusual lights; dealing with mad or stray dogs; cruelty to animals and children; lost property; suicides; and how to trap burglars by " marking " doors. This was done by using old matches, cotton and small pieces of mica. The idea was to stretch cotton across an entrance which led to a house with valuable property. In theory, broken cotton meant that a burglar had gone in. It sometimes worked, but I found that cats were no respectors of our devices to catch thieves.

It was during this intensive course that I first saw the

detectives. Our class was taken to New Scotland Yard, on the Embankment, and as I walked in I noticed the men lounging around the entrance, talking and smoking. They all had a quiet air of authority about them, and they all wore hats, mostly bowlers. One or two of them winked as we marched by, and then they suddenly disappeared. The reason was apparent a second later, when our sergeant saluted one of the Yard chiefs as he walked out. The detectives must have seen him first.

For two hours we were taken round the enormous building, shown the hundreds of thousands of record files, told how fingerprints are taken, and saw the rooms where the C.I.D. chiefs worked. When I reflect back on that visit we saw very little of the Yard, but it made me feel important, part of a giant, vital organisation with immense power.

At the end of eight weeks, despite trying hard to learn the million and one things, I felt uneasy at the final examination, but I passed, as did most of the class, and we went to get our uniforms, which consisted of one serge jacket buttoned up to the neck, two tunics made of fine cloth, one for ceremonial occasions only, a vast and heavy greatcoat with a belt, and an oil lamp, a helmet and a truncheon. We provided our own boots, and were allowed a shilling a week.

On the last day there was wild speculation as to where we would be sent. I fancied the bright lights of the West End, as did everyone else, or the fashionable area of Kensington or Chelsea. Instead I got the most notorious district of the East End, Whitechapel. Before I left the training school an old sweat said to me: " Whitechapel! Christ! They *eat* coppers down there." I did not know about Whitechapel then but I began to learn on December 29, 1919.

*   *   *

On the notice board at the training school I read my name: Peter Henderson Beveridge is appointed a police constable on probation. It was a great moment and even more exciting when I was given my warrant card, a small black-covered piece of thin cardboard which folded in the centre. When I opened it I could see that I had the same authority as any other policeman in London, for, no matter what rank is held, the powers of a constable remain the working basis of the Force.

I was ordered to report to Leman Street police station, just off the busy Whitechapel Road. It was my first excursion into the neighbourhood, a shabby, sour-looking world of grubby streets and mean dwellings. I went first to the section house, the home for bachelor policemen. It was a newish brick building from the outside, but inside clean enough with white-glazed walls.

Compared with today, the living quarters were primitive. On each floor were a number of cubicles with wooden walls that stopped about two feet from the ceiling. There was an iron bedstead, a hard chair and a steel locker with only a few shelves for clothes. At intervals down the corridor spluttered gas lamps so that only certain cubicles were reasonably well lighted. Mine was certainly not one of those, for there was a simple rule of the section house which allowed the old hands to take the best cubicles, or bunks, as they were called.

There were ninety-nine men there, all in the charge of a sergeant. He showed us the mess room, a place of strictly no comfort. There were five large scrubbed deal tables with a locker room adjoining. I was given one of these lockers and handed a key. " Keep your food in there," said the sergeant, " and keep it locked." I thought this advice a little unnecessary, after all, I was living in a police building, but I soon found that my brother constables were hungry and occasionally ran short of some vital commodity like bread or tea.

The duties of all " uniform men " were called: early turn, 6 a.m. to 2 p.m.; late turn, 2 p.m. to 10 p.m.; and night duty, 10 p.m. to 6 a.m. There were occasional variations which meant starting an hour later and working what was called a patrol.

I was told to parade the next day for early turn to start learning the beats. There were fourteen beats, which had to be worked in a certain way each day. Broadly speaking, one day the beat was worked clockwise and the next in the opposite direction. To be on parade at 5.45 a.m. it was necessary to get up at four-thirty, make some breakfast in the mess room, polish my boots and buttons, and, armed with all the notebooks, truncheon, etc., take my place in the long line of policemen waiting for their orders in the parade shed.

Our numbers were read out by the parading sergeant, we were inspected and then marched off, a long line of ambling blue-clad figures, turning off the line as we reached the start of the beat. I was told to work with a constable of many years' service who knew the area with an intimacy which comes only to one who has patrolled the same streets for years. Figures looked up in the darkness, said briefly, " Morning, Charlie," and were answered with " Hallo, mate." Charlie, who immediately christened me " Jock " because of my pronounced Scottish accent, explained who the people were. They included tram drivers, dustmen, quite a number of charwomen, street traders and lorry drivers.

As we wandered round, pulling padlocks and pushing doors, he told me something of Whitechapel. " This is a good place to learn to be a copper. If you can work here you can work anywhere," he said. " This is the easy shift. We'll get the kids across the road from half-past eight to nine and then have breakfast. We'll bring the little darlings back across the road at twelve o'clock and we'll put 'em in again at half-past one. If any of 'em get killed it's your fault. The rest of the time we keep our eyes open, look for thieves, stop the street traders taking up all the road and the pavement as well, ' nick ' a street bookmaker, if we're lucky, and tell a lot of cheeky chappies the time and the way to go. We also keep a very sharp look-out for the sergeant and the inspector in case they see us doing anything we shouldn't." He paused. " That's almost everything. Now, if they catch you, they put you on the ' rattle,' which means you have to appear before the chief and get told off or fined and that goes on your record. Then when you sit for promotion you might not get anything."

I found out later what good advice this was, for Charlie himself, a first-class policeman, had blotted his record with a few peccadilloes and was still a constable after twelve years' service. But men like Charlie were, and are, the backbone of the police force.

For two weeks I was taught the beats and then went out alone. The more I saw of the Whitechapel area the more unlovely it seemed. Nearby was Shadwell, Wapping, Limehouse, Poplar, Bow, Bethnal Green and Shoreditch. The streets were dark and dirty, forbidding thoroughfares with a variety and strength of smells which brought tears to my eyes. On every hand there was poverty and an amazingly cosmopolitan collection of races, many of them Polish and Russian Jewish refugees. There were also Lascars and Chinese, Indians and Scandinavians, who met, during the day, in hundreds of cafés with greasy, steamed-up windows which defied the penetration of the keenest eye.

The only different horizon for the local people was provided by the waterfront with its docks, wharves, cranes and ships. Years before, that waterfront had had its invasions of river thieves, gangs of men who hi-jacked boats coming in and stole their cargo. Now the River Police with their fast launches took care of any trouble on the Thames, while we looked after what happened on the banks.

In those days raids were made mostly from the land, for the London docks handle more than 60,000,000 tons of merchandise in a year, a rich prize for crooks. I learned how they worked from the other constables, how cases were pilfered and smuggled out in lorries or horse-drawn vehicles, how parcels would come out of the hold of a ship and mysteriously disappear into the rapacious hands of some receiver.

I soon discovered that the local inhabitants knew me for precisely what I was, a raw recruit. The children also realised it and began to mimic my accent. The street-corner boys—we called them " yobos " in those days—decided to obstruct every corner so that pedestrians had to walk in the road. I had been told what to do. A tough old sergeant warned me: " If you don't get in amongst those toughs they will run your beat for you. You may get a hiding, but you must do it."

The first time I lost my helmet, which rolled into the road, but the crowd dispersed. Next time I did not lose my helmet and arrested two of them for insulting words and behaviour. After that there was no more trouble.

In the early weeks I heard all about the famous Sidney Street siege, which occurred a few years before when two Lithuanian burglars, wanted for murder, were cornered in a house by armed police and troops.

Three weeks earlier these men had shot and murdered several policemen and injured others who surprised them in a jeweller's shop in Houndsditch. Then there were stories of Jack the Ripper, the murderer who prowled the streets at night claiming his victims from the local street women. I noticed that his depredations had in no way decreased their enthusiasm. Their customers were mostly seamen, and there were any number of brothels which catered for the men who came off the ships.

One of the reasons why the police were so busy was the great unemployment problem. Thousands of local men could not find work, and the hovels they lived in made the street a much better place in which to while away their time. Inevitably, these little crowds of men began to gamble, posting a look-out at either end of the street. We did not arrest many but merely stopped the games by walking down the street, and the gamblers vanished.

In two months I had come to know some of the people, their names and a little about their families. I also came to know a few of the criminals. Today, there are " local thieves' albums," but not in my early days. I discovered some of the local scandals, the habitual drunks, the old women who drank methylated spirits and collapsed in the street, and the married couples who fought every weekend and were quite prepared to hit each other with a bottle, or a broken glass, but still resented outside interference.

There seemed to be thousands of children—with parents who were either too busy, too poor, or simply not interested in caring for them. They were left to fend for themselves, to brave the streets in all weathers with totally inadequate clothing and roam about until late at night. Many youngsters I knew down there passed through my hands in later years.

Hardly a day passed that I was not called into one of their houses where there had been a fight, an accident, or someone taken ill. The squalor was unbelievable; sometimes whole families living in one room, often sleeping in one bed. Often the only tap for the whole house was in the

yard at the back. People with houses near the river told me
that their basements were always damp, frequently soaking;
and in the summer there was no ventilation. Overcrowding
forced them to spend as much time as possible in the
streets.

In practically every street stood a bookmaker, or one of
his touts, and there always seemed to be a steady supply of
small bets. This was partly responsible for the queue outside the pawnbrokers' shops on Monday mornings when the
sheets, or the pots and pans, or Father's best suit, were
pledged until the following Saturday, when they were
redeemed for the weekend, if Father brought home the
week's wages or, more usually, the dole. There was a never-
ending succession of tally-men (credit drapers and the like)
who thrived on the poverty of their clients and practically
forced them into any kind of sale, for few of them could
afford to pay cash. But, in spite of the squalor, they were,
in the main, hardworking folk, quick to help a friend
and ready to bring the spice of a Cockney quip to any
situation.

I made my share of arrests for drunkenness and the
frequent fights when the public houses emptied, but it
was not until March, 1920, that I had my first arrest for
crime. I was on night duty, when one is apt to dream more
than at other times of the day, for there is less to do and the
streets are quieter. The pubs were closed, the drunks
dispersed, and I was left alone to my lonely pavements and
padlocks.

About midnight, wearing my heavy greatcoat and
carrying my rolled cape, I sheltered from the keen wind in a
doorway. My old-fashioned oil lamp was on my belt but
turned away from the street.

Suddenly two men appeared, each carrying a large carton.
As they walked nearer I decided to stop them and stepped
out of the doorway. Startled—one swore blasphemously—

they threw the cartons at me and ran in opposite directions. I was fast on my feet in those days and managed to catch one after a quarter of a mile chase.

The cartons contained clothing later identified as having been stolen from a nearby goods depot. The second man was arrested later, and both were sent to prison.

I was elated by this success, and, encouraged by the fact that the first " Big Four " had been named, four men who to me at that time, and indeed later, had the glamour that film stars now have for teenagers, I applied to become a detective.

The " Big Four " were Carlin, Hawkins, Neil and the famous Frederick Wensley, known in the East End as " Mister Vensley " or " Pinwire," who had previously worked in Whitechapel and was now at Scotland Yard. He had investigated many murders and, indeed, had caught one killer when he was still a uniform man patrolling the beat.

I was commended for that first arrest and eagerly waited my chance to work in plain clothes. The system then was that a number of C.I.D. applicants were appointed each October to work as " winter patrols." (Now they are called Aids to C.I.D.) For that work we were allowed to dress how we liked, the overriding rule being that we must look as inconspicuous as possible. The rougher the district the rougher the dress, and sometimes we did not shave for days.

One of the most prevalent crimes at the time was thefts from the docks. Horse-drawn vans carried thousands of pounds' worth of valuable property every day and a crime known as " van-dragging " became popular. It was a simple scheme. The thieves waited until the van was going slowly, jumped on the back and threw off the parcels to a confederate before the driver noticed what was going on. Since most of the vans belonged to the railway we worked closely with their police, and it was then I met Detective Sergeant Dick Richards who afterwards became Chief of the British Railways Police.

With only nine months' service, I began work in plain clothes on winter patrol. Each year, from October to March, while the nights are long and dark, aspirants for the C.I.D. were selected to work in pairs and try their hands at thief-catching. If you worked hard and were lucky enough to make some good arrests, there was a chance of becoming a full-blown detective.

With my partner, a senior P.C., always called " buck " in the police, and dressed up in rough clothes, I patrolled for twelve hours a day. In those days there was much horse-drawn traffic and an enormous amount of property stolen on its way from the docks to the warehouses. Sometimes we hired, or borrowed, a horse and van and patrolled the streets in it, taking turns at holding the reins, something which incidentally neither of us had done before. Other times we climbed into the back of a van and surprised the hi-jackers as they pounced. In four months we had more than fifty arrests besides one or two other successes in finding men on the run from prison or wanted at other police stations.

In February, 1921, I was appointed a detective constable and, to my great delight, remained in the same division. The fact that I was delighted may sound odd, particularly because of the unsavoury neighbourhood east of Aldgate. But, as it had a fascination for Daniel Defoe, who sheltered from the Plague in its streets, and for many other mighty intelligent people, so it has a fascination for the police officer.

One good reason was that, in those days, most of the best thieves came from there. They were born to crime, nurtured in its barbarous arms, and pitchforked into the maw of the professional crooks who welcomed any apprentice with enthusiasm.

Working in the East End was a rough-and-tumble existence, where the civil answer was unusual, but where some of the people were not only fighting authority but battling against dreadful social conditions. They often compelled my admiration—they had courage.

CHAPTER THREE

PLAIN CLOTHES

STAYING IN THE same division was a distinct advantage. I knew the area fairly well and all the uniform men, my late companions of the beat. When I went down to the storeman to hand in my uniform he said: " Blimey, Jock, you're soon away. I fancied it myself once but there's too many hours in it for me. You wait until you're married —then you'll be in trouble." All that sounded vaguely discouraging, but I was too enthusiastic to worry about anything at that time. I came to remember his words later.

On my first day I reported to the divisional detective inspector, a mighty man of immense power, who controlled all the criminal investigation work. He shook hands with me and told me that I had been well recommended to him. " You know the area," he said, " and you may know some of the people, but you don't know much yet. This ground is full of good thieves, and so are all the neighbouring ' manors.' I want you to make as many arrests as possible, keep your reports up to date, study all the publications and orders, and don't neglect your duties. If you can get a few informants so much the better, but watch them."

" Thank you very much, sir," I said. Then, as I got to the door, he said: " One last thing. Always wear a hat— it's more dignified." I nodded, said " Yes, sir," and walked out—a full-blown detective.

I went to the office, where the junior detective was delighted to see me. With a broad grin he handed over all the publications of information. " Here's your first job,

Peter," he said. " Keep all these up to the mark and file them away each day. Very important job, this. The old man gets very shirty if they're not right."

I accepted the situation, knowing full well that, as the best cubicles in the section house went to the old hands, so the most junior detective was sure to draw the most boring jobs.

The day began at 9 a.m. and finished round about 10 p.m. The crime reports began coming in before we went on duty. Warehouse-breaking, thefts from vehicles, victims of pickpockets, shoplifting, assaults and burglary. My first job was a theft from a gas meter, little enough but a start. I went down to the house, a poor dwelling just off Aldgate. I knocked on the door and a woman's voice shouted: " Come in, mate." I pushed open the unlocked door to see a woman, quite young but careworn, sitting on a stool suckling a baby at her breast. I caused her no embarrassment, but it made me a little pink round the neck. I didn't have to introduce myself. " You from the station," she said. It wasn't a question, just a flat statement.

I asked her where the gas meter was and she pointed up to the passage, near the door. It had obviously been forced; there were eight families living in that house and an ever-open front door. What chance was there of catching the thief? Practically none, but the crime had to be recorded. I might get someone for it later, although it often happened that the people who owned the meter were so poor that they themselves broke it open to get some food. There were sometimes four or five of these thefts in a day but few arrests. Even so, the thefts, however small, had to be recorded.

I was gradually being introduced to the business of cultivating informants, more colourfully known as " stools," " snouts " or " grasses." With senior officers I went to certain public houses in the area to see who was about and prepared to talk in return for a drink or two. The D.D.I. had sent out a message that two gangs of shop-breakers who were breaking into tobacconists' shops and gown shops must be caught. These gangs had made hauls worth thousands of pounds and all we could discover was that each time they raided a gown shop a red-painted van was seen in the vicinity, and whenever a tobacconist was raided a horse-drawn van was seen around.

Six of us were assigned to the job. We had no transport, so we dressed up in the oft-worn disguise of old jacket, dungarees, cap and muffler and began to work practically round the clock. One of our inspectors had some infor-mation on the gang but we found that they had all deserted their usual haunts. Those of us who did not know what they looked like studied photographs until we could have recognised them anywhere.

For three weeks we worked but the gangs were still making their raids, although not so frequently. Then, at four o'clock one morning, we had that little quota of luck which must always go with successful police work. Four of us were within hailing distance in a side street off White-chapel Road. The red van we were looking for was out-side a gentlemen's outfitters, facing towards the main road, with the driver at the wheel. Slowly we began to edge towards the van, keeping close to the wall in the shadows. We did not need to talk to each other; we knew what to do. One of my colleagues was within a few yards of the van when he was spotted by the gang's look-out man, who shouted a warning. Four men came running from the shop. One detective grabbed the driver and the rest of us chased the others. There was a fight in the middle of the street, brought to a swift conclusion with our truncheons, and we had four prisoners. The boss of the gang got away that night. We could hear his footsteps receding.

We found the shop door smashed in and the loot packed

in sacks on the floor, ready to be loaded into the van. The four men were charged and then we set out to find the gang leader. We visited his relatives who, of course, said they knew nothing. However, we called on them repeatedly and also kept watch on the house. Soon we heard a whisper from one of the underworld " snouts " that the wanted man was living in a furnished room in Wapping. Knowing he was dangerous, we made a dawn visit and took him off, protesting, in his night-shirt covered by an overcoat.

He made a great show of innocence and denied ever being at the scene of the crime. Foolishly he overlooked the fact that four policemen had seen him run away, and he duly received his reward of seven years. The others were all found guilty and went away for varying terms of penal servitude.

The gang raiding the tobacconists' shops was still active although not confining its activities merely to our station area. It turned out to be another early-morning job, this time half an hour after midnight. As my " buck " and I turned a corner into Commercial Road we spotted the horse and van drawn up by the side entrance of a tobacconist's shop. We ducked into a deep doorway and watched. In the light of a street lamp we saw the glint of a jemmy and heard the metallic sound as padlocks were wrenched off the shop door. Then the three men went inside. We were a little surprised at that; it was unusual for a gang of three not to leave one man as look-out.

My colleague, a sergeant, whispered: " Come on, Peter. In we go." Together we sprinted silently along the road to the shop and grabbed the three men as they staggered out, each carrying a large carton of cigarettes. Then we realised why they had not left a look-out—the cigarettes had been delivered late the previous evening and left on the floor to be put away in the morning. As happens in so many cases, greed had overcome caution. They gave no trouble and walked meekly into the station. They all had long records and finished up with heavy terms of imprisonment.

I soon discovered that life as a detective was not always exciting. I had experienced the thrill of the chase, the man-hunt, which is more thrilling than any other sport. By using the word " sport," I do not underrate the seriousness of police work, but we are human and as much affected by atmosphere and circumstances as anyone else. As the climax of the fox-hunt comes when the quarry is cornered and killed, so the great thrill of the man-hunt is reached when the detective lays his hands on the man he wants. There is no particular personal feeling about making a capture unless the criminal has offended against the normal rules of decent conduct.

When mixing with criminals, you come to accept certain standards of behaviour. A good thief, who steals by cunning, and is caught or gets away, is not automatically considered a blackguard. The man who hurts, carries a weapon or makes women or children suffer can expect scant consideration from us. Those are not regulations but the judgments of the average detective who hunts with skill and enthusiasm but who, in certain circumstances, can also be a very ruthless foe indeed.

In my youthful ignorance I thought that I had left petty crime behind for ever and that now I was going to work on the more important cases. Instead my sergeant, next day, ordered me to concentrate once again on thefts from gas meters. I felt, rebelliously, that I was being punished. In fact I was being taught the hard way—and the right way.

So I went back to the interminable rounds of checking on hundreds of people, most of whom would have been glad to pick up an odd five shillings, and to try and find who was breaking open the gas meters.

I had an idea it was the work of young boys but could find no lead until one day I walked into a shop to buy some peppermints. The section house meal had given me indigestion. I knew the owner of the shop slightly and we stood and talked for a while. I asked him if trade was good, expecting to hear that it was the reverse because the neighbourhood was extremely poor. He said: " Well, guv'nor, it's not at all bad. The kids seem to be getting money from somewhere and they are spending with me."

" Any particular kids? " I asked. " No," he said evasively. " I don't think I would know any of them. I don't know if they even come from round here."

I knew that he did not propose to give me any information and realised that I had put my question too quickly. I admired him for his reticence but knew that his young customers might be the answer to my problem. I decided to watch the shop and thanked him for his help.

He looked unhappy when I walked out. I was not very happy either, but crime has to stop, even with children. I waited for the next wave of gas-meter thefts. They happened one evening and were reported about midnight. I was at the shop when it opened at seven-thirty next morning.

In less than half an hour a young boy, aged about ten, walked in. I followed and stood by the door. I heard him ask for some bars of chocolate with nuts and raisins, a fair purchase for those times. I met the boy as he came out, a pleasant, fair-haired, freckled-faced kid who, as I took his arm, said " Leave me alone," and shook off my hand. " What do you want? "

" I just want to speak to you, son," I said.

" What about? "

" About the money you used to buy those things in your pockets."

" I ain't done nothing; you leave me alone," he said.

Gradually, as we walked along, he softened. I told him who I was and, before we got to his home, a basement dwelling in one of the many mean streets, he told me that he had taken the money from a gas meter at one of the addresses that had been reported. In the end I found out that he was but one of a gang of eleven who had been stealing for months. He told me some of their names, and when I saw those boys, usually in the presence of their schoolmasters, they gave me some other names. Eventually I found them all.

They were all charged, found guilty and bound over to be of good behaviour. That chance visit to the sweet-shop, the indigestible lunch, was the means of clearing up more than fifty cases of theft, and the books at the station began to look much tidier.

I was frequently in court, giving evidence, and the people who thronged the public gallery came to know me, like those in the streets who had little else to do but watch for " the law," as policemen are always called in the East End. It had its disadvantages but also prevented many a young man from straying from the path of righteousness. Their parents got into the habit of asking me, and some of my colleagues, to give their children a stern lecture. We did this willingly, and quite a few of those youngsters who had once hovered on the brink of the criminal merry-go-round were stopped short.

Another advantage in being fairly well known was that informants became easier to find. I met one by an odd chance. He walked into the station and asked for me. I had never seen him before. " Will you buy me a drink? " he said. I was tempted to chase him off but, for some reason, said: " Yes, I'll buy you a drink for your nerve." Over a glass he said he had heard about me from some other people, mentioning no names. He thought he could put some " jobs " my way. I had nothing to lose and told him to telephone me at any time he had anything good. When he left he said: " I reckon you could advance me five bob, guv'nor, couldn't you? " It was against all the rules, but

I gave him the money, and told no one else at the station. They would have called me an idiot.

Two nights later the telephone rang for me. " That you, guv'nor? " said the voice of the man who had "nipped" me for five shillings. " Beveridge here," I said, in my best official voice. He went on: " There's a load of ' pussies ' (furs) in the fourth shed in the alley behind the goods yard. The boys are taking a buyer there at ten o'clock tonight."

That was at eight o'clock. I, and two others, were there fifteen minutes later. Just after ten, three men arrived, opened up the shed and went in. We gave them a couple of minutes and followed. The man who had been brought down to buy the furs was examining them, the other two standing by. " All right," I said. " You're nicked (arrested)." It was one of those occasions when explanations are not needed. They accepted the situation but refused to say where the furs had come from, and later that night I found that they had been stolen from a West End store by shoplifters. I brought the surprised owner down to identify them, and the three men were charged with stealing and receiving. They went to prison but still refused to disclose the names of the shoplifters.

While I was in the East End, I came to appreciate the worth of the Criminal Record Office. Many times a week I went up there with nothing more than a description of a man or woman suspected of some crime. Usually I saw an old sergeant who had been in C.R.O. for more than twenty years, and he may have realised that I considered him as a lesser mortal because he was doing an inside job while I was investigating outside. He used to say with irony: " Well, Jock, don't tell me you have come to us for a little help." I knew he was a good-natured character and I always asked politely for information.

" I'm after a woman, middle-aged, who is working a

false pretence on the ground. She's taking orders and deposits for stockings for a firm that doesn't exist."

" Well, my son, we have about ten thousand of those. Which one would you like? A little more description would help, you know."

I came to understand just how magnificent this department was. They had every crime listed and every person who committed crime neatly filed under a variety of headings. I came to know the Photo Albums room, more commonly known as the " Rogues' Gallery." He showed me the books of pictures all listed under description and types of crime. " Supposing you want a robbery with violence merchant, aged about twenty-five, five feet six inches tall. We look up the Index and find the group of men in that category. There are twelve pictures, front and side, on a page which you can show to any witness. By showing the whole page the identification is fair to the man who may be accused. The witness is given no suggestion as to which of the men, if any, is suspected. That testimony will stand up in court.

" But it may be," he went on, " that the witness can't give enough description and only remembers that the robber had a wart on his nose, or a scar on his face, or a twisted finger. Then we turn to the Deformities and Peculiarities Section. Under all crimes are listed the crooks known to have certain odd things about them.

" Supposing it's a con-man with a broken nose. He's using a false name, so a name search will mean nothing." He pulled open a drawer. " Here is the con-men drawer and there are thirty-two with broken noses. All right, you haven't caught him yet, but he may be one of thirty-two, which is a start. A few more details and he's yours—with any luck.

" Then you can try Method Index, one of the most useful. Criminals don't change their habits or their methods. They can change everything else, except their fingerprints.

Take the fellow who poses as a domestic servant of some kind. He may be a butler one day, a cook the next, or perhaps a gardener, but he always uses the same method of first getting into the house in an innocent guise and then stealing from the inside."

I saw the amazing lists of crimes, many of them new to me. There was everything from Arson and Assault down through the alphabet to White Slave Traffic. On each card is the date of birth of the offender and his height. The classification goes further and tells the investigator the favourite " character " assumed by the criminal. There are Agents (a very common title), Actors, Foreign Diplomats, Gold Miners, Doctors, Charity Workers, Journalists, and dozens more. The methods used are listed in detail. There are men who pose as electric-meter inspectors to gain entry to a house; women who purport to collect for charity; men who dress as clergymen and feign illness to steal; burglars who always help themselves to a meal before leaving. Everything a criminal has ever done in the course of a crime is carefully recorded.

I realised then how important were the reports we had to type, the reports which we thought were a dreary nuisance and kept us at the desk for hours when we pre-ferred to be out catching thieves. The detectives in C.R.O. depended on the information they received from the investigating officers. The more they recorded, the greater the help available when another crime was being probed.

Before I left that day, the sergeant told me: " Remember, son, criminals don't change their ideas. They may get better at whatever they began but a safe-breaker won't turn into a pickpocket, and a fraudsman won't go into the smash-and-grab racket, although he might turn to forgery. In the same way a robber (theft with violence) might go in for burglary but he won't try the confidence game."

I was impressed by this department and used it on many

hundreds of occasions later, and seldom did it fail to help in some material way. Even so, I did not relish their job of catching thieves on paper only, and hoped, secretly, that I would never have to work there.

Soon after that informative visit to C.R.O., I met Edward Greeno, now Chief Superintendent. He, like me, was a detective in the East End and we began to work together. We were about the same build, slim, but well able to handle ourselves in a rough-house, and our one aim in life was to arrest as many criminals as possible. A prevalent offence at that time was pickpocketing. These men worked in small teams in any place where crowds collected. One was the tram terminus in Aldgate High Street which served the farthermost parts of the East End. The pickpockets concentrated on Friday evenings, pay night, and Greeno and I joined the crowds. We were dressed like City workers and, after a few minutes, saw four men who looked like pickpockets jostling in the crowds. We watched and, as the people surged towards the empty trams, the four men moved with them, relying on the victims feeling nothing owing to the pressure of bodies all around them and their eagerness to fight their way on to the tram. We were behind the four and could not see exactly what they were doing, but as they reached the step of the tram they turned away and broke free from the crowd. We followed and arrested them as Suspected Persons. They all had convictions for stealing from the person—in other words, " pickpocketing."

We caught many more pickpockets at Aldgate and also in the busy markets. Then we were told to concentrate on a different type of theft, that of women stealing from drunken seamen. This always happened after the public houses were closed. These women, who had met the seamen in the public house, would lure them into a dark back alley on some amorous promise, steal their money and run away. Some of these sailors had more than £100 on them after a long voyage.

Greeno and I watched the people leave a certain public house and followed one couple. The man was being half supported by a woman and they disappeared down an alley. In less than five minutes the woman walked out, tucking something inside her low-cut blouse. We stopped her and asked for the money. She was so surprised that she took out a wallet and only then began to cast doubts on our parentage. We found the sailor lying dead drunk and arrested him for drunkenness and the woman for theft. Next morning at court the man remembered nothing except that he had had a large sum of money. He was discharged on pleading guilty to being drunk and the woman was sent to prison for six months. The magistrates took a most serious view of this type of offence and usually gave the maximum. One night Greeno and I managed to catch five of these women between 10.30 p.m. and midnight and that also helped to check the practice.

In those days I rarely wore a decent suit or a clean shirt, for nearly all the work was keeping observation on some crook or other, and rough clothes were essential. I remember once walking into the station canteen at Arbour Square, Stepney, dressed in a seaman's jersey, a muffler and a cap, stained trousers and filthy, down-at-heel shoes. I had not shaved for at least a week. In the canteen was another man from Fife, Station Sergeant Alec Miller, who was having a drink with a friend of his from St. Andrews. I was introduced and we talked for a while. I noticed the visitor looking at me rather closely but thought it was pure inquisitiveness. A week later, my father wrote to say that an uncle of mine had heard from a friend who was visiting Mr. Miller that I was looking very rough and untidy and he was concerned for my prospects in the police force. My uncle had made a special journey home to impart this vital

family information.   My father, of course, immediately
understood the true situation and explained to his apprehensive brother-in-law that detectives do not necessarily
have to dress like dandies.

The informant I mentioned earlier was still supplying
me with odd tips, and it was he who first taught me how
dangerous they can be. One afternoon I was called into the
detective inspector's private room. He looked grave and I
wondered what I had done, my mind making a lightning
back-flip on the events of recent weeks. The inspector's
words were as grave as his mien. " Beveridge, there is a
nasty complaint against you. Yesterday, a man walked into
the shop of a receiver of stolen property and spoke to him
about a load of leather he had bought cheaply and which he
knew had been stolen. The shop owner admitted it and the
visitor identified himself as Detective Beveridge."   The
inspector looked hard at me and went on: " The man who
gave the name Beveridge said he could square the whole
business for a consideration and he took twenty pounds for
not arresting the shop owner. I must tell you that the
description given does not fit you. Who can it be? "

" What does the man look like? " I asked. The inspector
read out the description and I knew at once. It was my Irish
informant who so liked a drink. I was relieved and told the
inspector. He said: " Well, you had better find him. Drop
everything else."

I needed no urging. If I could have met that man whom
I had always known as " Mick " I would have knocked
him cold.

It took me two weeks of anxious searching, and then, one
evening, I saw him in one of his old haunts, a public house
in the Whitechapel Road. He had been away from the area
all that time, spending the money he had received by using
my name. I grabbed him and told him why. He denied it
strenuously but, although he had shaved off his moustache,

I was fairly sure. I took him to Leman Street Station but still he declared his innocence. He was left to cool off for a while before some senior officers took him to Bethnal Green Station for interrogation. Fifteen minutes later they telephoned to say he had confessed and the reason he had not done so to me was that he was afraid of what might have happened. He was a reasonable judge of character!

That episode taught me a valuable lesson. Informants are useful and necessary, but dynamite. They must be given no chances and no quarter if they go wrong. Certain sections of the public are only too willing to believe the worst of any police officer and such complaints are, quite properly, investigated. The guilty officers are not volunteers and, indeed, they try every trick to appear busy at some other job. Even so, officers are commanded to watch their fellows, and they are known throughout the police as the " rubber-heel mob." They were often stationed in the East End but seldom there for long without being noticed. One man, I remember, so resented being put on the job that he wore a police athletic club tie and was instantly recognised.

*　　*　　*

By 1926 I had passed all my examinations and was almost due to be promoted. The Whitechapel and Stepney areas were in a ferment owing to the great industrial depression, and there were frequent fights. Then, at midnight on May 3, 1926, came the General Strike. Public transport vanished and the streets were crowded. Newspapers shrank to single sheets and volunteers began to drive buses, trains and trams. All police leave was stopped and we remained on permanent duty at the station, sleeping whenever we could. The Yard sent us a news bulletin every day and we heard that a bus had been overturned at Hammersmith, but we had our own troubles. A crowd of malcontents smashed windows in many buildings and we arrested more than forty of them.

Criminals soon began to use the strike to their own advantage, breaking windows and stealing from shops.

There were riots throughout the day in all the main roads and the mounted police were frequently called in to break up the crowds with their long batons. Unfortunately, they had difficulty in distinguishing between rioters and detectives and several times I narrowly missed a clout on the head.

On May 12 the strike was over and we returned to normal duties. I took some back leave to go home to Scotland and it was then that I met the girl who became my wife. She was born not far from my home and our courting had been mostly by letters between London and Scotland, and reinforced by occasional holidays. I made up my mind to marry, if she agreed, when I became a sergeant.

CHAPTER FOUR

SOHO AND MAYFAIR

I HAD TO wait another two years for promotion, but, by then, had managed to rid myself of being in charge of official publications. Even so, the years on that job were invaluable. Every day these police " newspapers " are sent out from the Criminal Record Office and printed at the Yard. The most important, the *Police Gazette*, is circulated to forces throughout the country and contains details of persons wanted, suspected of, and in custody for, crime, particulars of property stolen and persons missing, of bodies found, and aliens who have contravened the restrictions. There are also various supplements dealing with expert criminals, details of prison releases of certain classes of offenders and any re-conviction of those persons. More than 7,000 copies of that " newspaper " are printed every day.

In addition, there is a confidential paper known as *Information* which deals with methods used to commit crime and persons suspected but not identified. Many times I have read through *Information* and seen a crime method being used elsewhere which was precisely the same as the case I was investigating. Someone from another station, probably miles away, had a suspect. It was a reasonable supposition that the same man had committed both jobs, and by reading *Information* I too had a likely suspect and knew whom to look for.

There were lists of stolen cars, and Pawn Lists which gave descriptions of jewellery and other expensive articles lost or stolen which might be offered for sale at a pawnshop or jeweller's. Quite frequently there were amendments to the law which had to be entered in the appropriate book, and also a Special Inquiries Register. These special inquiries are an important part of C.I.D. work and are usually requested in cases of serious crime and, almost always, in murder.

There was the time, in September, 1927, when P.C. Gutteridge, of the Essex Constabulary, was shot dead while on night duty near the village of Stapleford Abbotts, not far outside our boundary. It was one of the most callous and brutal murders ever committed.

The P.C. was shot in the head twice while he was lying on the ground, dying. A strange car had been seen that night in the neighbourhood and the investigating officer immediately asked for a special inquiry to be made at all garages for a car of that description. The car was found by police in Brixton shortly afterwards and it provided vital clues to the capture of Frederick Browne and his partner Kennedy.

In many cases the victim of a crime cannot be readily identified but there may be a laundry mark or a cleaner's tab on the clothes. Accordingly, a special inquiry is made to establish identity through the laundry registers. It is but part of the thoroughness which is the main plank of police success. Most of the " intuitive " detectives are only to be found in works of fiction.

Browne and Kennedy were hanged in May, 1928, and it was about that time that sinister rumblings came about police corruption in the West End. In fact, in that same month, Chief Constable Wensley, former chief in my division of the East End, had been instructed to probe these allegations of bribery which concerned, in the main, clubs, gambling dens and brothels. Mrs. Kate Meyrick ran the famous 43 Club in Gerrard Street at the time, a place of which I had heard but never entered. This probe finished up with the suspension of Sergeant Goddard and was fol-

lowed by his arrest and appearance at Bow Street charged
with three others in conspiring to pervert the course of
justice. If the arrest was sensational, even more so were
the facts which came to light. Goddard was found to have a
house worth £2,000, a luxurious car, bank deposits, and was
renting safes with safe-deposit companies. It was later
revealed that he had more than £12,000 in cash hidden away.

Goddard was sentenced to eighteen months' hard labour,
fined £2,000, and ordered to pay the costs of the prosecution. Mrs. Meyrick and Luigi Ribuffi were both sentenced
to fifteen months' hard labour. The fourth person in the
conspiracy had fled the country and did not stand trial.

The people of Whitechapel read of this trial with keen
interest. They were quite happy that there was a " copper "
in trouble and lost no time in saying, in general: " He's
only *one* that's been caught. I always said they were all
crooked." Some went farther and shouted " Goddard "
at us, but always from a safe distance. We all had a pretty
good memory for faces and those who were sufficiently
injudicious to shout were " seen " quietly. The shouting
stopped.

Crime was on the increase, one major reason being that
unemployment was growing more serious every week.
People were in a mood as sour as their surroundings and,
as a consequence, the police generally were busier than ever.
I was doubly delighted, therefore, when my promotion
to sergeant came through in May, 1929, and I was posted
to King's Cross.

My new station was different from Whitechapel only in
that there were fewer foreigners. There was certainly no
shortage of criminals, and we had one or two gangs of
toughs who intimidated bookmakers on the racecourses.
Street bookmakers flourished like weeds despite the poverty
that was evident all around, and the queues outside the
Labour Exchanges were depressingly long.

I had been there but a few months when a new type of crime developed, known to the police and the underworld as " blagging." The idea was both simple and brutal, and it is still used today. The thieves found out when, and where, messengers collected large sums of cash from the banks, followed them for a few days to find out the exact route they took and then attacked them, having first stolen a car and parked it handy for a quick getaway. They had the most useful element of all on their side—surprise— and they often carried heavy coshes.

We had a fair idea of the ringleaders of this gang but could get no forewarning of a raid until one Thursday evening, when I was having a glass of beer in the station canteen, a constable told me I was wanted on the phone. It was one of my informants, who said: " There's a job tomorrow morning, at Clerkenwell Green—it's the wages from the bank." He mentioned the name of the firm and the bank.

I knew the narrow little street and realised we could never watch on foot, so we decided to keep observation from an old covered van. We were there, four of us, at nine next morning, parked where we had a good view all round from slits cut in the sides of the van. Almost an hour later a dirty van, quite small, turned into the street and stopped about thirty yards away. When the messenger left the firm to go to the bank one man got out of the van and followed him. Then two others arrived and went to the van. They seemed to be doing something with a large sheet of newspaper. Then they walked towards the bank each carrying a piece of newspaper and showed it to another man who was idly looking in a shop window. I caught sight of something red and realised it was jam on the newspaper which they were going to smack over the messenger's face and snatch his bag with the wages.

Here was a problem. If I let them make the attack I

would catch them literally red-handed at robbery, but the messenger might be seriously injured, even killed. I decided there was enough evidence, anyway, and issued my instructions. As soon as we saw the messenger approaching, we left our van. The thieves did not even see us for they were too intent on watching their victim, and we grabbed them with the messenger only three yards away, happily oblivious of what was waiting for him. Another of my men had cut off the escape of the van driver, and we bagged six prisoners. Inside the van was a half-empty jar of jam, not at all the quality the bank messenger would have enjoyed.

When the thieves were sentenced at the Old Bailey to long terms of imprisonment the case was neatly summarised by a tall City policeman who remarked, as the men were led down to the cells: " Jam today, but porridge (prison) tomorrow."

*　　*　　*

On my annual leave that year, 1930, I went home to Scotland and was married at Fife. My old colleague of the Whitechapel days, Sergeant Tom Johnson, was best man and our section-house sergeant, Charles Saunders, was a guest. I had previously managed to find four rooms over a shop in the Caledonian Road, not far from Pentonville Prison, and there we moved at the end of August. Within two weeks of settling in, my wife had a first taste of the rigours of marrying into the C.I.D.

About four o'clock one morning we were awakened by a loud banging on the downstairs door. I went down and found one of my colleagues, Detective John Ball, now deputy chief of my last district. He told me that a newly born baby had been found, alive, wrapped in a newspaper, in a warehouse doorway in a side street off Farringdon Road, Clerkenwell. The child had been taken to hospital and was expected to live.

We waited an hour for dawn and then went to the doorway where the bundle was found. Close by, we found a trail of blood. I had already examined the newspaper in which the child had been found and there was no blood on it, so it looked as though this blood must have come from the mother, which presupposed that she had not received any medical attention. The trail was fairly heavy and we followed it easily along the street and up a flight of steps to another street and from there to another, smaller street, to a doorway. We thought our quest was at an end but, after interviewing every person in that house, drew a blank. We carried on again with our search of the pavements and roused the occupants of several houses in the vicinity who were quite happy to tell us what they thought of being disturbed at that time on a Sunday morning. Then a woman, walking along the street, said " Why don't you try over there? " and nodded towards a doorway. We went across and there saw a few spots of blood. A heavy knock on the door produced a young woman, very pale and blonde, and obviously making a terrific effort to appear at her ease, but it was clear that she was ill. I told her we were policemen and she asked us in, then sat heavily on the stairs. In a weary voice she said: " Can you fetch my sister? " With the sister's help we got the woman to her room and put her to bed. A few minutes later the ambulance arrived and she was taken to hospital.

A search of her room gave us all the necessary evidence. It was a sad case. The young woman was married but her husband had been abroad for a long time and was not the father of the child. She had become frightened and tried to abandon the baby after suffering the ordeal of child-birth without any medical help. Fortunately she recovered and so did the child, and they were restored to each other. Later the woman was charged but received a most

The author's father

P.C. Beveridge

The author as a Seaforth Highlander

Plain-clothes Detective Beveridge

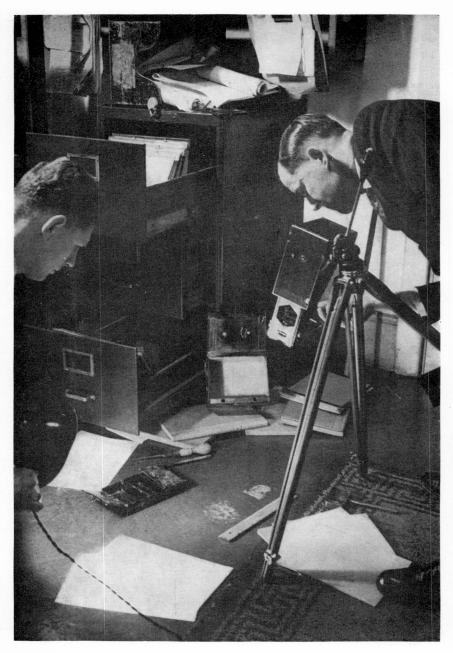

The Photographic Branch in action at " the scene of the crime "

sympathetic hearing from the magistrate, who placed her on probation.

My wife was shocked at that case but soon became used to the odd things that happened in London, even when a particularly scruffy informant decided it would be safe to call to see me at home. My wife hardly believed that he had come to see me or that I wanted to see him, but she took the message and passed it on. From then on the same man always gave me his tips that way, but never managed to get past the front door, which was, perhaps, just as well.

In 1934, the Flying Squad was in the charge of the famous Chief Inspector Dan Gooch, and I was delighted to be transferred to him on promotion to detective inspector. At that time, the Squad, sometimes known as the " Sweeney Todd," was equipped with fast cars and radio but all messages were sent in Morse and it was not possible to transmit to the Yard from cars. For that reason most of the radio operators were ex-naval signallers and they sat in the car with headphones, decoding the messages. Any communication with the Yard had to be done by telephone.

I soon realised that the Squad was a much-feared body of detectives. They were tough, clever and unorthodox with a terrier-like ability to shake a case until every prisoner was arrested. There was Jerry Lynch, Ted Powell, " Chesty " Corbett, Frank Drew and Cyril Woodcraft, all master detectives with an amazing knowledge of criminals in various parts of London.

I remained on the Squad only six months but there were two jobs typical of the daily round. One afternoon I took my car to South London and, when passing a quiet garage, saw three notorious criminals in a commercial van. When they left the garage we were on their tail and, for a while, went round in circles with them, they trying to see if they were being followed, while we made sure that they remained ignorant of our presence.

4—CID

We kept tailing them while another Squad car, in charge of Cyril Woodcraft, joined in, with each car taking turns in leading.

The suspects turned off towards Guildford and on we went into the country. The van stopped and one man got out to look at a large house. That happened several times in half an hour and suddenly we came face to face with them round a sharp bend. The van had been drawn into the disused drive of a country estate and the three men gave up without a struggle.

In the van was a complete set of housebreaking implements and the entire floor covered with a mattress to ensure the comfort of whoever looked after the van while the others did the stealing. Their next stop was a cell in Guildford police station and then Wandsworth Prison after several cases of housebreaking were proved against them.

*   *   *

Serving in the East End at that time was a young detective named Stephen Glander who is today a chief superintendent occupying my old office. He telephoned one day to say that he had a tip that three men had planned to break into a shop somewhere in the West End. Their plan was for two of them to get into the empty premises next door and force an entry into the shop on Saturday, stay there all night and gather the loot together. On the following morning the third man was to pick up a taxi at a certain café in Frith Street, Soho, at nine o'clock and drive round to the shop. There the three men would bring out the parcels and the taxi driver would not suspect anything.

I decided that Glander would work on the job with Sergeant Ted Renson and myself, and we arranged to keep watch from a taxi. Promptly at nine o'clock a smartly dressed man, slightly in the style of the American gangster, walked out of the café and hailed a taxi. He had a good look round before he got in and was driven off. We followed through the side streets into Piccadilly, then into Duke Street where it turned round and stopped facing the other way.

We had to drive past, go quickly round the block and park where we could see them. Their taxi was outside a high-class gentlemen's outfitters and we were just in time to see our suspect knocking on the side door. It was opened immediately and he stepped inside. Three men walked out, carrying large parcels which they loaded into the taxi. We let them make three trips and then dashed for them. The man we had tailed saw us coming and in a flash, without giving his mates any warning, ran into Piccadilly and disappeared.

A look at the premises convinced us that the job had been done according to the original plan. The two men who had been inside had taken down large stocks of the best-quality goods and parcelled them up ready to take away.

At Vine Street the inspector welcomed us with the enthusiasm one expects from the recipient of a Littlewood's cheque. He had good reason, for several similar jobs had been pulled on his ground, although in a different area.

Shortly afterwards I was sent to work in the West End at Great Marlborough Street, which included half Soho and half Mayfair, and in those days it would have been hard to find two districts more contrasting. In Soho, we had the criminals meeting in the shady clubs, and the respectable tourist public; in Mayfair, the aristocracy and the fashionable hotels. Only one thing was common to both areas— the ladies of desire. They, too, seemed aware of their surroundings, for those in Mayfair kept a little decorum and asked higher prices while the Soho variety were often drunk and disorderly. It was a time of prowling killers who took these women as their prey. Not long before, Dora Lloyd had been killed in Maida Vale, strangled by an unknown man who had been heard but not seen. She, like most of her kind, lived in a house where night noises are not unusual, so that her screams were not remarked on until the killer was on his way downstairs. Even then the man who heard them decided it was none of his business and remained in bed.

There had been other cases, all strangulation, which gave a brief moment of glamour to the sordid women who were described as French Paulette, French Fifi and French Marie. Norah Upchurch had been murdered in the same way and her killer was still unknown.

*   *   *

There were nine C.I.D. officers at that station and I think it was the happiest time of my career. The work was heavy but it was fun, because the uniform men and my detectives worked so well together. This liaison was perfectly illustrated when we had a heavy case of shopbreaking in Bond Street. The thieves appeared to have entered with a false key and taken a large quantity of ladies' dresses. They had taken so many that a vehicle must have been used.

I asked the men on the beats if they had seen anything suspicious over the weekend. Less than an hour later, a constable came into my office and produced his pocketbook. He showed me some notes he had taken concerning the actual address in Bond Street and also, even more important, the names and addresses of three men. The constable had seen the men loading gowns into a large van and, when questioned, one of them showed keys to the shops and satisfied him that they were genuine employees. Nevertheless, he had also taken the number of the van.

I called at the shop and found, to my astonishment, that these three men had given their correct names, for two of them were known to the proprietor and had at one time been employed at the shop. Furthermore, one of the men had been allowed to keep the keys while he was employed there. It seemed fairly certain that he had taken an impression.

Another detective traced the index number of the van to a cartage contractor in Wapping and I went down to see him. He told us he had been engaged to remove the goods and had taken everything to an address in Soho. He came with me in the car and, at the address mentioned, we found all the stolen property and three receivers. Later we captured the three thieves. A happy end to that story is that the constable, who alone had made the job possible, was soon afterwards promoted to sergeant.

Those of us who were in the inner divisions of London at that time missed at least one most arduous job, that of watching for the famous burglar " Flannelfoot." He had started operations about two years previously and by then had achieved considerable notoriety. He was really a small-time thief but a consistent worker. He raided mostly small terraced houses on Saturday and Sunday nights by pushing up the window catch with a sharp instrument or by removing the putty and taking out the window-pane. Sometimes he manipulated the door key, conveniently left in the lock, with a pair of fine pliers. He left no fingerprints and also covered his shoes with flannel to leave no prints.

Detectives in the outer divisions kept observation for months on end and we tried to get a line on him, but without success, for he worked entirely alone and stole mostly cash. Two years later he was caught, just when I was sent back to my old hunting-ground, Whitechapel, as the divisional detective inspector.

In the same year Chief Inspector Fred " Nutty " Sharpe handled the fascinating murder which began at St. Albans and moved back to the West End where I had been so recently. The body of a man was found out there in

Hertfordshire and the flashy clothes, pointed patent shoes and manicured hands suggested that he had been dumped there.

The man had been shot six times, in the chest, back and side; his face was scarred with old wounds but had been recently battered by a fist. He was soon identified as Max Kessell Allard, a man whom I had known in the West End as " Red Max," always something of a mystery to me and my officers.

Chief Inspector Sharpe, an amazing man who once arrested nine pickpockets on a bus by the simple expedient of telling the driver to go straight to Bethnal Green police station, soon traced Allard back to a house in Little Newport Street, Soho. He had gone there with a woman and been shot dead by her lover, George Lacroix, over a debt of £25 which he owed her.

Both were arrested in France and tried there for murder. At the trial it was established that " Red Max "Allard was a white-slaver who sent girls to the Argentine and let furnished flats for immoral purposes. The woman was acquitted, and Lacroix sentenced to ten years on Devil's Island.

Whitechapel was quieter, so far as crime was concerned, but there were other troubles; Blackshirt troubles. These mobs, so named because of their Fascist uniform, who followed Sir Oswald Mosley's political beliefs, and therefore those of Hitler, were determined to exact some real or supposed vengeance on the Jews.

There were mass meetings almost every night which deteriorated into brawls and fights, then wanton damage and woundings.

One Sunday afternoon motor-cars were overturned and set fire to, and almost every Jewish shop had its window broken and the contents of the shop strewn over the road. That day we made seventy-six arrests.

These political troubles had been going on since 1934 and they increased in gravity. At one point, in 1936, the Old Street magistrate, Mr. F. O. Langley, said: " I want to make it clear that there are only two sides to this controversy —those charged to maintain the peace and those said to disturb it. Whether they are Communists or Fascists, or anything else, does not matter to this court. This mischief is getting beyond limits and more drastic steps may have to be taken."

Rarely a day passed without minor or major riots which involved some serious injury to at least three or four policemen. A crowd of 2,000 once gathered in Bethnal Green after a Communist meeting. More than 100 policemen were on duty in the area.

This anti-Semitic disease spread by Mosley threw its germs into many hundreds of hitherto quiet citizens, who suddenly decided that all Jews should be baited and beaten up.

This dreadful cancer, which was working so successfully in Germany at the time, caught on in London. One Englishman charged with smashing two shop windows belonging to a tailor agreed that the shop owner who was being intimidated said: " You Christian—I dare you to break my window."

Damage became so serious that the insurance rate rose from one shilling to the £100 for twelve months to five shillings. That applied only to the East End of London.

There was never a political meeting which did not develop into a near riot. Men and women were hurled through shop windows; men were arrested in possession of bayonets, women with heavy sticks. The Fascists, 4,000 of them, marched through Stepney bearing a pig's head nailed to a banner carrying a red, white and blue flag. This was a purely provocative symbol and it caused the usual hostile crowd to collect and more arrests were made.

In my short time back there, in the East End, I must have handled more than 400 arrests, almost all connected with crazy politics, and then, fortunately, I was transferred back to the West End. It was like going from the jungle to apparent civilisation.

CHAPTER FIVE

DEATH IN DOVER STREET

EARLY IN 1938, when the international situation was beginning to take the shape of war, I was moved from the East End to the glamorous part of London looked after by the famous Vine Street police station, which has now become (I think, unhappily) the Aliens Office, a mere registration bureau. In those days Vine Street was the best-known police station in London. It was a boast of under-graduates that they had spent the night there for some " rag " on Boat Race Night.

The station, an old building of red brick, was tucked away in a quiet cul-de-sac behind Piccadilly Circus. From the outside it looked pleasant enough, even prosaic, but it was the busiest station in London. I went there in charge of the C.I.D. and I governed a fascinating area which stretched from the luxury of Park Lane, through Mayfair with its millionaires and plush hotels, across Regent Street into Soho, a square mile of restaurants, clubs—dubious and otherwise—film companies, pubs and disorderly houses. It was, and is, deservedly famous for its food and drink. It was rather more notorious for its vice, as common to Soho as the smell of garlic.

I had not been there long and was just settling down when the first of the Irish Republican Army outrages hit my area. We did not know, when the first explosive went off in a pillar box, that it had been placed there by soldiers of the I.R.A. with a grievance against Britain. All I knew was that bombs of all kinds began to explode in the thickly populated area under my command.

One evening, there were five big explosions in banks and post offices around Piccadilly and a number of civilians were injured. I gave orders for increased vigilance by all ranks to search anyone looking suspicious or carrying a parcel which might contain a bomb. I brought more men out in plain clothes.

Previously, two men had been arrested by the C.I.D. at Ilford. They were both Irishmen and in possession of a large quantity of explosives. Despite frequent and close interrogation, they refused to talk or give any information about their masters, and they were finally sentenced at the Old Bailey.

It was clear, and the detectives of the Special Branch confirmed it, that the I.R.A. were determined to make demonstrations to air their age-old political grievances against this country. Hardly a day went by without some kind of explosion.

I remember one date particularly, Saturday, June 24, 1938. Crime was quiet that morning, and at lunch-time I collected my wife and daughter and went to the wedding of an old friend and colleague, then Sergeant Jack Diller. After the wedding I went home with the firm intention of staying in for the rest of the evening. Less than an hour later, the telephone shrilled me back to work. It was Inspector Bob Fabian calling to say that there had been some I.R.A. activity and he thought I might like to come along to take charge.

My fast car took me to Vine Street, and as I walked up the stairs I was nearly suffocated. The whole place was full of smoke and the passageway streaming with water. I saw a uniform man through the smoke and shouted: " What the hell has happened? " He answered: " I don't know, guv'nor. I think Bob Fabian is trying to fire the station."

Some time later I learned that Fabian had been called to Piccadilly Circus, where a home-made bomb was sizzling away in the gutter outside the Chinese Restaurant. While two uniform men cleared the crowds away, Fabian grabbed the bomb and put out the fuse. In those brief seconds he probably saved hundreds of lives.

When I got to my office and put my head out of the window in order to breathe, I asked Fabian: " If the bloody bomb was in Piccadilly, why is the station full of smoke? "

He laughed. " I brought the bomb back to the station, but I forgot to put it in water. It caught fire again."

Fortunately there was no damage, and later, on my recommendation, Bob Fabian was deservedly awarded the King's Police Medal for Gallantry.

My detectives arrested several of the small I.R.A. operators, who were sentenced to varying terms of imprisonment, but we never got near the men who were directing a campaign which might well have resulted in wholesale murder.

Even so, the threat was considered so serious that at least twenty extra men were drafted to my division each evening. I posted some of them at various strategic points and kept a reserve at the station so as to get to any trouble spot within a few minutes.

Normal crime continued. There were burglaries in the wealthy district of Mayfair; bank messengers slugged on the head and robbed. The pickpockets were active in the busy streets when women were doing their shopping; confidence tricksters were happily bamboozling their wealthy victims in the best hotels; and thefts from cars were too frequent for my comfort. There were plenty of arrests, but even detectives have to sleep sometimes, particularly when working an average of fourteen hours a day.

Then war, which had been threatening for so long, burst upon the London scene. Every decent citizen was worried and unhappy about a future that stretched uncertainly ahead, although they did not know then how bad things would become. The criminals, however, were delighted. They were confident of shortages on which they could capitalise, and they knew there was to be a complete black-out, a useful cover for operations.

I got my informants to busy themselves in the underworld to find out what plans the criminals were making. One source, from which I heard plenty, was the women who disgrace the pavements of so many streets in the heart of London.

One of these women proved to be the victim of the first murder investigation I handled alone.

These girls were of all nationalities, some French, many English, some Irish, some Welsh, some even German, but all the foreigners had, at some time, gone through a marriage of convenience. They had paid a sum of money, anything between £20 and £50, to go through a wedding ceremony in order to acquire British nationality. They lived in expensive and, in some cases, luxurious flats, many of them in and around Bond Street or Dover Street and all quite near Piccadilly. They did well enough, most of them, to employ a maid and live in considerable luxury.

Prostitutes, of course, take their lives in their hands. They are seldom selective as to their company, and every time they take a client to their flat they are taking a chance, which they accept as part of the hazard of easy money.

One girl, whom I had seen many times in the Dover Street area, was pretty young Iris Heath. That was the name we knew her by, and whenever I or my colleagues were around in the evening, any time up to the early hours of the morning, she would be there standing on one of the street corners, smartly dressed, smoking a cigarette. Sometimes she would be chatting to another street woman, but most frequently talking to men.

Early in February she was standing in Dover Street. It was cold and she had her collar turned up to keep out the

chill wind. There were few people about, but towards
11 p.m. a slim young man walked along the pavement
towards her. He noticed Iris, for she was wearing a smart
black hat and red costume. She walked across the pavement
and they chatted.

The man walked back with her to a house in Dover
Street and together they climbed the stairs. In the flat
she began to tell him she owed the rent and money to
several other girls. The man, now comfortably settled in an
armchair, said: " I'll give you some money if you will
play the game and be decent. Why don't you stop, before
it's too late? "

" I can't," she said. " I work for some people. I've
gone too far."

" What's your name? "

" Iris," she said and then went on: " Would you like to
stay the night? I owe so much rent and I need money
badly."

" Yes, I'll stay," he said, handing her a five-pound note,
which she tucked down inside her blouse. They talked and
smoked for a while and then ran out of cigarettes. She
volunteered to get some and he gave her a pound note.
She soon returned with a packet of cigarettes. Five minutes
later, the woman with whom she had been standing on the
street came in with a small bottle of whisky and asked Iris
if she was coming to have some food.

" Aren't you going to stay with me? " asked the man.

" Yes, I'll be back in twenty minutes." She left the
flat, after giving him a drink.

The man waited half an hour and then, feeling tired,
climbed into bed. When he awoke it was six o'clock and he
was still alone. He waited for four hours and then the front
doorbell rang and he heard a man's voice shout: " Is
anybody there? " He opened the door and the man said:
" What are you doing here? "

" I'm waiting for a young lady," he said.

" There is no young lady here. I'm the landlord. An elderly woman lives here."

He had now been in the flat for twelve hours. He was confused and annoyed and the poorer by £6. He walked out and went home.

That little cameo of the West End was nothing unusual. The Mayfair ladies were notorious for their methods of getting money from young men by playing on their sympathy, but that particular evening's work was the prelude to murder, my first as chief of the C.I.D. in the West End.

About ten o'clock, three nights later, a man walked into Vine Street and reported to the station officer that he had found Iris Heath dead in her top-floor flat in Dover Street. I took Inspector Fabian and together we went to the flat. I pushed open the door and there was the girl I knew as Iris Heath.

Her body, nude apart from an underskirt around her neck, was lying about eight feet inside the door. There was a stab wound in her chest, near the left breast, and she had been bleeding from the nose and mouth. Several of the dentures in her mouth had been broken and some of the teeth were lying on the carpet. There was also a stab wound in her back, near the top of the left shoulder, similar to the one on the chest, and blood-stains blotted the carpet. Just inside the door was a double bed on which the bed-clothes were also heavily blood-stained; it did not appear to have been slept in. There were blood-smears on the floor behind the door which looked as though they had been caused by the dead woman's body being dragged to where it was found.

In the same room was a white blouse, turned inside out, with blood-stains which looked as though a knife had been wiped on it. On the carpet, inside the door, was a woman's brassière and a corselette still fastened. All those clothes were blood-stained and they had all been ripped up the front with a knife. With these things was a woman's stocking, which had also been cut from below the knee to the right back suspender to which it was attached. The left back suspender had been torn off and was lying underneath the eiderdown with a piece of stocking attached. On the back of a chair was a reddish-brown coat and skirt and a pair of knickers.

" Looks like her last client, Bob," I commented.

" Yes. She had obviously taken some clothes off and the client cut the others off. Looks as though he used the knife to stab her, too."

" Ring the Yard, Bob," I said. " Let's have the print and picture boys round. And ask them to contact Sir Bernard Spilsbury."

While Fabian went out to the telephone I took a look round the room. At first sight it looked as though the woman had fought briefly with her attacker.

With my colleagues I searched the room without disturbing anything but could find no trace of the murder weapon. While Sergeant Law, now Superintendent in charge of the Photographic Branch of the Yard, was taking his pictures and the fingerprint men examined the room I began my inquiries.

Through the Criminal Record Office I discovered that the woman I knew as Iris Heath was also known as Georgina Hoffman. She had several convictions for soliciting but had been in no other kind of criminal trouble. She was well known in the area and popular.

The next step was to find when she had been last seen alive, a difficult fact to discover in such a part of the West End and with such a woman. Her " colleagues " had always been slow to talk and seldom like interfering in any way or assisting the police in an investigation. They have a dislike, possibly understandable, of the police and are always reluctant to be dragged into a murder investigation.

I discovered that Georgina Hoffman was a married woman and rented the flat at £6 a week and that she had a friend who also worked as a prostitute in the same area.

The man who had called at Vine Street to tell me of the murder was a Mr. John Roman. He had gone to the flat at the request of the dead woman's friend, and I sent out one of my sergeants to bring her to the station.

Meanwhile, I had ten detectives on the job making inquiries all over Soho. I quickly discovered that Mrs. Hoffman was born in Wigtownshire in Scotland in 1912 and that her husband lived in Finsbury Park. A message was sent to the nearest police station and he was warned to come to Vine Street at once.

Sir Bernard Spilsbury arrived at the flat about midnight. He greeted us with his usual courtesy, put on his white apron and stood for some minutes surveying the room, taking in every single detail. Then he examined the body and made a note of the wounds, studied the fingernails, the wrists, and the abrasions on the face. Then, and this is the only time I ever saw Sir Bernard Spilsbury do it, he got on his knees to make a minute examination of the carpet. It was interesting to watch this man, whose superb dignity had impressed courts all over the country so many times, the man who had been referred to as " the incomparable witness." There he was, in what was for him an undignified posture, kneeling on the floor with his magnifying glass before him, studying what could be, in any murder case, vital evidence. To me, as the detective in charge, it was of inestimable value to have a man like Bernard Spilsbury on my side. He, in his own right, had solved many cases, so I knew when he went to the witness-box that his evidence would carry tremendous weight. When he finished, I saw him downstairs to the door, escorted him to his car and bade

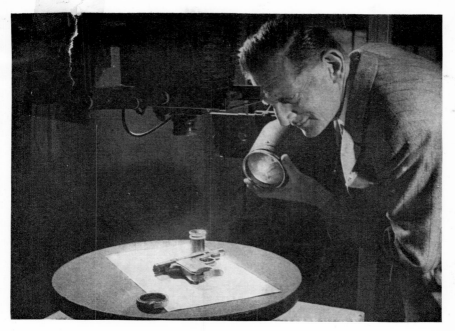

Taking a close-up of an automatic pistol left by a criminal

Examining clothing for dust with a special vacuum cleaner attachment

Recruits at Hendon Training School study procedure of making an arrest

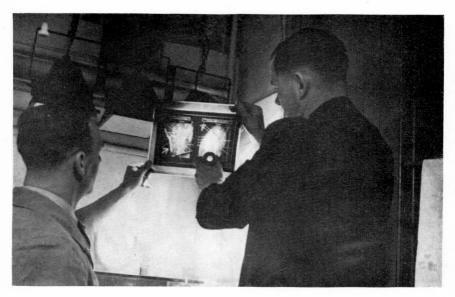

Fingerprints are a detective's best friends

him good night. Then I carried on with the inquiries to find the man I sought.

I found out that Mrs. Hoffman had taken the flat on February 4, saying that she intended to stay for only two weeks. This was obviously false, because she had no intention of returning to Scotland and, indeed, had been following her profession for some time, certainly long enough to have been convicted ten times.

I went back to the station and found Mrs. Hoffman's girl friend waiting with Inspector Fabian. She was hysterical and did not want to talk even though her friend was dead. After a while we calmed her and she gave me the first real lead. She told me that, early on the morning of February 10, she had called at Mrs. Hoffman's address. She asked her to come out, but Iris had made an excuse, saying: " I've got a client upstairs; he's given me five pounds and he wants to stay the night. I don't like him; he talks funny, as though he hasn't a roof to his mouth." She had told her not to let him stay if she didn't like him but to take him some whisky and leave him. " Tell him you are going out for some supper."

A little later the friend went up to the flat. She saw a man there, sitting in a chair, reading. She described him as aged about twenty-eight years, five feet seven or eight inches in height, slightly built, fair complexion and with brown hair. He was dressed in his shirt-sleeves. She noticed his peculiar speech, and after a few moments left the flat with Mrs. Hoffman, leaving the man there. That night the victim stayed with her. On the evening of February 10 she saw her in Dover Street with the same man. She said on that occasion: " Is he all right? " Mrs. Hoffman replied: " I think so."

She watched the two of them go into the flat in Dover Street and next saw Mrs. Hoffman about midnight on the same day. She told her that the man had no money but that

5—CID

she had his watch and he was going to give her £5 for it on the following night. She showed her a wristlet watch which, as far as she could remember, was of white metal on a chrome strap with a buckle and with something peculiar about the hands and the face that she thought she would know again. Mrs. Hoffman told her friend that the man was going to meet her at ten o'clock on the following night to give her the money. That night the women went home together to Kingston and came up to Town again on the following day, soon after noon.

On the Sunday Mrs. Hoffman's friend remembered seeing this same man with the peculiar voice standing in Berkeley Street. She had jumped out of a car and asked where Iris was. The man replied: " I haven't seen her." She had understood he was to have seen the victim the night before but he said he hadn't. She was still talking to this strange man when Mr. Roman came back after having discovered the body. She could see by his face what had happened and shouted: " Don't let him get away. He was supposed to meet her last night."

They all adjourned to a restaurant, and Mr. Roman then went for the police. Asked if he had anything on him to show who he was, the stranger said he hadn't, and wrote his name on the table. Somebody picked it up before he walked away. She remembered that the man had written: " Arthur Layton, 62 Broomgrove Grove, Clapham." I had checked, but, as I expected, it was false.

This statement was corroborated by another man who was present, and from it we got a very fair description of the man who was possibly the murderer and certainly worth interviewing. But first we had to find out who he was.

This was another occasion when the Criminal Record Office rendered me invaluable service. At 4 a.m. I sent all the witnesses down to the little witness-room at the place the newspapers call the Rogues' Gallery, and they gave the sergeant in charge their idea of how this man looked. They were carefully cross-examined on points of height and colouring, and, after a short while, the sergeant produced pictures and allowed the witnesses to see them. It is worth explaining here that, to form a useful identification parade, there must be at least seven other people of a similar height and description as the suspect to make the parade absolutely fair.

In this case we were assisted by the fact that all the witnesses said the man had an impediment in his speech, possibly a cleft palate. In the special section under the heading of " Peculiarities," under the sub-heading " Speech Impediment," all people with records of violence were turned up. One was found whom the witnesses identified as Arthur James Mahoney. From his criminal record, it was established that he lived in Hargwyne Street, Brixton.

At nine o'clock on the morning of February 13, having been working for twelve hours non-stop, I went with Detective Inspector Long to Brixton and saw the prisoner. That is always a fascinating moment in a detective's life, when he is face to face with the man he thinks he is after, the suspect who may eventually die through his evidence. It is also the moment for great care. I said: " We are police officers. What is your name? " He replied: " Arthur Mahoney."

" We are making inquiries respecting the dead body of a woman found in a flat at Dover Street, Piccadilly. You answer the description of a man recently seen in her company. Can you account for your movements on Saturday night last? "

" I don't know what you are talking about," he said calmly.

I walked in with my colleague and, whilst Mahoney stood in a corner, we searched the house. It was not long before we found some evidence to support our belief that the witnesses had been right in picking him out. In a cupboard in the kitchen was a blood-stained shirt. I said: " To whom does this belong? " " It's mine," replied Mahoney.

Inspector Long searched him and from his right-hand jacket pocket took a wristlet watch and from the left-hand trouser pocket a blood-stained handkerchief.

Things were beginning to add up and, by this time, we were certain this was our man. But there was more to do yet, and I continued to search the house.

When I was in the kitchen Mahoney called us into the passage and said: " Don't tell Mother, and I will tell you where the knife is." I cautioned him in the well-known phrase: " You need not say anything unless you wish, but anything you say will be taken down and may be given in evidence." He said: " Come upstairs." He went to the chimney in the back bedroom and pulled out a knife in a leather sheath, saying: " This is what I done it with, she tricked me of all my money." I examined the knife and there were blood-stains on the blade and the handle. Mahoney seemed quite composed, and, indeed, glad that he was about to be arrested. I told him that I was going to arrest him and take him to Vine Street police station. " I will tell you why later," he said quietly.

When we got to Vine Street he told me the whole sordid story.

Mahoney, who was twenty-three, was an engineers' steward on board ship. He arrived in London on February 7, and went home to his mother at Brixton. Two days later, his prelude to murder began. He had a little over £6 in his pocket. By next morning the dead woman had tricked him out of most of it, and his mind turned to violence. He was determined to see the woman again and his thoughts were in strange conflict. He wanted to reform her but he also wanted to get his money back. He bought a

sheath knife at a shop in Coldharbour Lane, Brixton, with
the idea of frightening her both into returning his money
and to show he was in earnest about wanting her to go
straight. He waited in the street and saw her pick up
another man whom she took to her flat. In fifteen minutes
she returned alone and he went with her to her flat. He
was upset about seeing her with the other man and told
her he loved her. She said she felt the same but would
never go straight now. He tried to leave the flat but she
asked him to stay. There came a ring at the doorbell.
" It's the landlord," she said. " Have you got the money
you promised me? " " No," he said, " I haven't."

She flew into a rage, went to the door and returned, still
furious. She swore at him and started fighting. He pulled
the knife and struck her.

Mahoney was excited now, almost as though he was
re-living that moment of murder. " I lost my head. I
pushed her on the bed and we were still fighting. The bed
was fully made with the eiderdown on top. I then noticed
blood coming from underneath her armpit. She was still
fighting with me and screaming. I got alarmed and tried to
quieten her with pillows over her face. Eventually we
rolled off the bed and, as we did so, the knife fell on the
floor, so I picked it up and struck her again. She was still
struggling with me.

" This time I struck her on the chest, causing the blood
to come. She was then lying behind the door moaning:
' Arthur, I love you. Kiss me before I die.' I tried to pick
her up and put her on the bed but found she was too heavy,
so I dragged her to the foot of the bed and left her there.
Whilst lying there she kept moaning: ' Arthur, Arthur.'
This upset me so I decided to leave her for what she was.
I ripped her clothing and stocking off her body with the
knife. When I left she was still moaning. Before I left the
room I wiped my knife on one of her undergarments, put it

in the sheath and walked home with it in my pocket, as I had
no money to ride. I got home about half past one in the
morning. Before leaving the flat I took my watch from the
drawer in the dressing-table."

At first sight this appeared to be a difficult murder, but,
as often happens, and it did in this case, a very few hours
were required to clear up the whole thing. When the
inquiry began there were certain people, mostly people who
get a precarious living from the streets of London, who did
not want to talk. They never do want to talk, but sometimes, particularly in a case of murder, they eventually
decide that they will tell what they know. In this case,
having once got a description and a name, and, in particular, knowing the man we wanted had a cleft palate, we
passed the inquiry over to the Criminal Record Office at
the Yard.

A few weeks later Mahoney appeared at the Old Bailey
and the defence pleaded insanity. This failed and he was
sentenced to death. Within two weeks, however, he was
certified insane and sent to Broadmoor, where he died not
long afterwards, in July, 1940.

*   *   *

Meanwhile, we had problems with gangsters, who
terrorised the neighbourhood and lived on what they called
" protecting " bookmakers' pitches on the racecourses and
dog tracks, and who also organised crime. These men
occasionally became news, when one of their confederates
was razor-slashed or beaten up, but their clashes were
usually confined to themselves and seldom harmed the
general public. These wounding crimes were difficult to
probe because the men who had been attacked almost always
refused to reveal the identity of their assailant, and any other
witnesses were similarly dumb. Whenever I went to see one
of these thugs who would perhaps have a six- or seven-inch

razor scar on his face the reply was roughly the same: " Do me a favour, guv'nor. I did it shaving. I'll see the other fellow later," and that was as far as I got.

A few months prior to the start of the war a crowd of these terrors, or " tearaways " as they styled themselves, began to give trouble in the clubs, demanding money and drinks and smashing furniture when they were refused. I heard that the leader was one John Mullins, known as " Dodger," whom I had known in the East End. He hailed from Bethnal Green and was violent in a crowd, like most of them, but a craven when alone. I found out which public house he was using and, one evening, wandered in and stood beside him. He was startled to see me and even more shaken when I told him why I had come. " I hear you are invading my ' manor ', Dodger," I said.

"Your 'manor'?" he said. "Not me, guv'nor. You know I wouldn't do that. I don't even know where your 'manor' is."

" Well, I'll tell you, then you won't make any more silly mistakes, will you? "

He countered by asking me to have a drink. I took a large whisky and then told him the boundaries of my area, with the warning that if I saw either him or any of his gang there would be trouble.

From that time on they disappeared and peace was restored.

CHAPTER SIX

TEA FOR FOUR

IN JANUARY, 1940, I was promoted to Chief Inspector and given charge of the Flying Squad. I was delighted with this new appointment, because it had come swiftly and I had previously served for six months on the Squad as an inspector and knew some of the workings. The Flying Squad is the greatest specialist outfit in the Metropolitan Police, and the detectives who serve on it are chosen for their intimate knowledge of London's underworld. It was first created in 1919 with only twelve men, and originally formed to combat a new type of crime, the smash and grab. When it began there were only a few tenders out in divisions, which were used for getting to the scene of the crime quickly. When I took charge of the Squad, or the " Heavy Mob " as it is called by the criminal fraternity, there were fifty men and eighteen high-powered cars.

These men on the Flying Squad work an average day of about sixteen hours. They get no extra money, no large expense sheet, but they have the most fantastic *esprit de corps*, and are imbued with a spirit almost of recklessness. They are wildly enthusiastic and entirely dependable. Their home life is completely neglected because of the demands made on them. When ordering men to carry on for still more hours of duty I used to feel that they must have had divine guidance when they chose their long-suffering wives.

There were some well-known personalities in the Squad in those days, including such men as Detective Inspectors Greeno, Dance, Black, Capstick and Ball. Those five officers had an immense knowledge of London and the dangerous criminals who worked there.

My appointment to Chief Inspector meant also that I was now a member of the Murder Squad and on call for any provincial murder when the assistance of the Yard was requested.

In those days, in the early part of the war, crime came to London with explosive force. A black market such as Britain had never known was quickly organised, and the blackout gave thieves the opportunity for which they had been praying. The Squad headquarters at that time was a place called the Bungalow, a low building just inside the main gates of Scotland Yard. That was our home, our office, and the place where so many coups were planned. On paper the Squad worked in shifts; a dawn patrol, a late patrol and a night-duty patrol. In fact, it frequently happened that all these patrols merged into one, lasting about sixteen hours.

One of the early problems was created by deserters from the Forces, hundreds of whom were running wild in London. None of them could obtain food or clothing, or indeed earn any money by legitimate means, for everything was controlled by the identity card and coupons. Foodstuffs were short and things like cosmetics, toothpaste, clothing and silk stockings were hard to come by honestly. Gangs of thieves, backed by the deserters, decided to cash in on the situation. They preyed on London like wolves, stealing whatever they could. They specialised in stealing from railways, from lorries, from the docks, from warehouses and shops, and of course from private houses. The blackout gave them ample opportunity, and they were further helped by the fact that uniformed police had many other wartime duties.

It is an absolute truth of police work that where there are thieves there are receivers, and the war created a vast legion of them, not previously criminal receivers, but now prepared to buy almost anything in short supply and at inflated prices.

*   *   *

The Flying Squad has no boundaries and can operate anywhere in the 735 square miles of the Metropolitan Police area. While the blackout assisted the criminals, it hindered my men very considerably. Our cars had to travel with dimmed lights and quite frequently there was enforced radio silence for twenty-four hours, which meant that every car was operating independently and could not be contacted from my office.

One of our early troubles was handbag-snatching, particularly in the West End of London. Case after case was reported from the Charing Cross Road area and all around Theatreland. I planted detectives to watch, but here again the blackout made things difficult. But one night a girl, a little more courageous than the rest, was attacked and her handbag stolen. There was a telephone nearby and she ran and dialled 999. One of our cars happened to be passing and they picked up the girl and took her quickly round the streets, but she could not see the man they wanted. Then they went back to where the attack had taken place and searched every café still open. In one a man was comfortably drinking a cup of tea and going carefully through the stolen handbag!

Almost on the same date that I was appointed Chief Inspector of the Flying Squad, a famous criminal known as Ruby Sparks made a daring escape from Dartmoor Prison with another man called Nolan. It was almost as though Sparks had celebrated my appointment, and I was equally positive that I would, if possible, celebrate it myself by having him arrested as soon as possible. But I had to wait for a while and concentrate on the smash-and-grab raiders who had begun to work again in the West End. Shop after shop in Mayfair was smashed open early in the morning and thousands of pounds' worth of property, mostly jewellery, stolen. This problem became so acute that I got men from the local stations in the West End to concentrate on certain streets near Regent Street in the early hours of the morning.

It was not long before we had some success. One morning a uniformed officer telephoned to say that he had seen three men in a high-powered car in the Regent Street area. Two of our cars went up at once, but by the time they arrived the gang had smashed a window. The same uniformed man who had tipped us off managed to grab one of the criminals. Meanwhile, one of the Squad crews had seen another car in the vicinity, and it was to that car that the other two members of the gang ran in the hope of getting away. The Squad driver pulled his car round in front of theirs and forced it to stop. One man ran into a house and, shortly afterwards, came out of another door to be confronted by a War Reserve policeman. The man shouted " He's in there " and pointed into the house. The crowd shouted " That's him " and the P.C. grabbed him. I found an interesting bag. There was William Hill, now the self-styled " Boss of the Underworld," Harry Bryan and Georgie Ball, all of whom were part of what was known as the Kentish Town Mob. That was on June 25, 1940.

One day later, one of my inspectors, Mr. Greeno, received a tip from an underworld informant that Charles J. Sparks, known to us as " Ruby," was in touch with his well-known girl friend and accomplice, the " Bobbed-hair Bandit," and had arranged to meet her on June 27 outside the Ritz Cinema at Neasden. We knew where the girl lived, at a house in Wembley, and that evening she was followed from her home to the Ritz Cinema, where I had several men planted under cover. It was not very long before the redoubtable Ruby walked along the street and came to greet his girl friend, standing there in the shadows. All my men converged at once and Ruby was a very surprised housebreaker that night.

He had been out for nearly six months, a record break, and although he must have been absolutely shattered by our appearance, he managed to grin and accept the situation philosophically, and gave no trouble. I suppose, on reflection, he had little chance of giving any trouble, for there were enough detectives around to arrest at least ten Ruby Sparks. I spoke to Ruby at some length. He was quite pleasant and knew perfectly well that I suspected him of many crimes. All he would discuss, however, was how he got away from the " Moor " and how he lived when he reached London. Then he closed up like a clam.

Soon after that we caught another mob of smash-and-grab experts, this time from South London. They, too, were working the West End, and a Squad crew who had been keeping observation in the Mayfair area saw them make their attempt at a shop window, and pounced. They caught two, including the famous Charlie Gibbs, while a third, well known by the name of " Frani " Daniels, managed to escape but was picked up later. That for the time being stopped that particular offence.

Every day on the Flying Squad brought a new problem, and the next I had to deal with was the gangs who were specialising in breaking into country houses. All the targets they had chosen so far were on the outskirts of London in lonely districts and vulnerable to skilled house-breakers. Some of the gang members concentrated on " casing " the house to see what was there, and how it could best be entered. They managed to gain a great deal of information about the house and its occupants from local pubs and tradesmen, and then waited for a convenient evening. I organised two squads to work on this problem, and then suddenly the opportunity for which I had been waiting arrived in the shape of a provincial murder.

This took place six months after I was appointed Detective Chief Inspector. I had known for some weeks I was first on the list to go out, and was looking eagerly forward to the new experience. I had already selected the sergeant who was to accompany me, an old and tried colleague, Albert Tansill, with whom I worked many times afterwards. There was no shortage of Flying Squad work, but all the time I was waiting, and secretly hoping, that the call to a provincial murder would come. It did—on July 9 in 1940. I had been on duty all day and returned to the office with Detective Inspector Ted Greeno, now Chief Superintendent, who was then my second-in-command. That was around eleven o'clock at night and we were thinking of going home.

As we walked into the office, the duty inspector came up with an odd smile and said: " I've news for you, sir." He handed me a long message from the Chief Constable of Kent, Captain Davidson. I read the message, which described briefly the finding of the bodies of three women in an orchard at Matfield, near Tonbridge. The Chief Constable had asked that Scotland Yard be called in to assist him. I knew then that it was my job. Greeno, who afterwards made many brilliant investigations into murders, put out his hand. " Good luck, Peter. I'll look after the Squad while you're away."

The duty inspector told me that Detective Superintendent Alex Bell, who was in charge of the Yard's Central Office, had ordered me to take up the inquiry at once. I was very thrilled and, despite my twenty years in the service, a little excited.

I went into my office to telephone the Kent County Police and spoke to Inspector Fred Smeed, now Chief

Constable of Newport, Monmouthshire, and he told me more about the case.

It appeared that, earlier that day, the three bodies had been discovered in the grounds of a cottage at Matfield, about seven miles from Tonbridge, by the gardener of a relative of two of the dead people. It was suspected, he said, that two of the women, mother and daughter, had been shot in the back with a revolver, and that the other woman, the maid, had been bludgeoned about the head. So far as he could tell, the murders had taken place that afternoon. I realised then that I was already about eight hours behind.

Inspector Smeed went on to tell me that the women were Mrs. Dorothy Fisher and her nineteen-year-old daughter, Freda. The third woman was the maid, Charlotte Saunders, aged about forty-eight. Mrs. Fisher occupied a cottage with her daughter and Miss Saunders, whilst her husband, Lawrence Fisher, lived at a farm at Piddington, near Bicester, Oxfordshire, about eleven miles from Aylesbury.

I discovered that the Fisher family were known to the Chief Constable of Kent and his officers owing to the fact that an alien male friend of Mrs. Fisher, living in London, had quite recently been refused permission to visit Matfield, which was then a protected area. This was due to the war precautions which laid down that certain large areas of the South Coast were out of limits to certain civilians and open only to Service personnel.

The refusal by the police to give permission to this alien to visit the area had apparently caused some annoyance to Mrs. Fisher, and her husband had even made a protest to see what could be done. One last and important thing Inspector Smeed mentioned was that neither Mr. Fisher nor the alien gentleman had been seen by the police.

I decided to see both these men at the earliest possible moment. I got their addresses, collected the Murder Bag, which is no part of fiction, but indeed a very necessary piece of equipment for a murder investigator, and called for my car.

You will remember that at the time—July, 1940—the Battle of Britain had just begun and the Germans were manning their invasion barges across the Channel. The Nazi Air Force was particularly active over Kent. A total blackout had been enforced, and even the police could not break it, which, from my point of view, put me at a considerable disadvantage.

While I was talking to Inspector Smeed in Kent one of my constables telephoned Bert Tansill and sent a car to fetch him. He arrived very shortly afterwards, a tubby, fat-jowled, confident and extraordinarily efficient sergeant who later became a Chief Inspector under my command.

We jumped in the car and went off to see the alien, a Dane, accompanied by Detective Inspector Albert Smith, the night-duty Squad inspector. This alien lived in a comfortable flat in West London. I broke the news to him, and both Tansill and I were sure that his shock and upset were genuine. For a few minutes he could not talk, but then he completely satisfied me as to his movements for the whole of July 9. Even so, on any investigation, particularly murder, one cannot be too careful, so I searched his flat for firearms. There were none, and I was satisfied that at least one suspect was removed from my list. Tansill took a short statement before we left.

At this time my wife and my daughter were living in Berkshire and I had lodgings in Kensington. On the way back from seeing the Dane, I picked up a bag with a change of clothing and told my driver, Jack Frost, with whom I had joined the police, that I had decided to take my official car and he was to drive. It was a tiny matter but, oddly enough, it had never happened before. Usually the investigating officers went by train and used a local car, but I decided on this occasion, and for the first time, that in view of the blackout problem and the difficulty of finding my way around the countryside, my own car and driver were essential.

It was too late that night to ask permission, so it was not known at the Yard until the next morning. There were one or two stormy telephone calls asking me, " What the hell do you think you're doing, Beveridge? You get a car down there. Don't take our cars from here." However, I managed to ride the storm and stuck to the car, and, as events turned out, it proved a happy move.

July 9, 1940, was a Tuesday. I found out that Mr. Fisher left his farm each morning at eight o'clock and drove into Aylesbury, where he boarded the London train; apart from being a farmer, he was in business in the City. It was therefore necessary for me to be at Bicester before eight next morning. I was determined to be there if at all possible, and as time was getting short—anything could happen in those days to delay us—I arranged with the local police to stop Mr. Fisher on the main road away from the farm just in case I was not there on time. Jack Frost was probably the best police driver at that time and we were but a few minutes late. When I eventually arrived, Mr. Fisher was already speaking to the uniformed sergeant and wondering why he had been stopped.

He must have been considerably shaken to see a large black car, very obviously a police car, pull up and two equally obvious detectives get out. I spoke to him quite briefly and he satisfied me as to his movements on the previous day. I suggested that he should accompany me to Matfield to identify the three bodies. I was, of course, proposing to learn the whole background of his married life.

Before going on to Matfield, I suggested that I might have a look round his farmhouse and inspect any firearms he might have. He agreed readily, and with Tansill I searched the farm. I was going through the house, room by room, and in Mr. Fisher's room there were two beds with a woman in one of them. I had only to raise an inquiring eyebrow and Mr. Fisher explained that she was a Mrs. Ransom, a friend of his. She was not feeling well and had decided to stay in bed. Here was an interesting circumstance, I reflected, as I wandered around. It was clear that the woman was no stranger and, presumably, in the habit of sharing Mr. Fisher's room.

While Sergeant Tansill was speaking to Mr. Fisher and taking a few notes which might be useful at a later stage in the investigation, I wandered around the farm to get my bearings and see if I could pick up any sort of lead. Later, I was very pleased that I did. In the course of my wanderings, I talked to one of the servants who was of rather above average intelligence and I soon gathered that he did not approve of the set-up there. According to him Mrs. Fisher was very domineering and dictatorial. By " Mrs. Fisher " he referred to the woman I had seen in bed. According to the servant she had been living there for some time.

I had started with a completely open mind, and knew practically nothing of the background of the family. This servant seemed to be anxious to talk, so I let him. He realised that a visit from detectives at that time of the day was unusual, and he told me that for a week or two the woman had been learning to fire a shotgun which was owned by the cowman, and he had also been teaching her to ride a bicycle. He added that she was not very much good at riding it.

This was a great piece of luck, which is not always forthcoming in a murder investigation. I had stumbled on to something which was possibly of tremendous importance, but I did not realise then just how vital it was. All I was doing was collecting every possible fact, half-fact, suggestion or suspicion, in order to fit the jig-saw together. I

6—CID

appreciated, however, that the servant seemed frightened of the woman and his remarks might be prompted by malice.

When I returned to the farmhouse I was surprised to see, standing there with Sergeant Tansill and Mr. Fisher, the woman whom I had seen in bed in the house, this Mrs. Ransom. She was dressed in blue slacks and a fancy-coloured sweater, and I noticed, indeed I could not have missed it, that she had a mop of red hair. I also saw that she used cosmetics quite extensively, and that her fingernails were painted bright red.

I was introduced to her by Mr. Fisher and we had a brief discussion, mostly about the weather. I gave Tansill a look of warning and made no mention of the position at Matfield. She waved to us as we left for Tonbridge, accompanied by Mr. Fisher.

As we got into the car, Tansill whispered to me: " I'll raise the subject of the family. Very interesting." We sat in the car and Tansill, addressing himself to Mr. Fisher, said: " Can you tell us about the Danish gentleman? I understand he has been refused permission to visit Mrs. Fisher at Matfield because it is a restricted area." I was not quite sure what Tansill was up to but guessed that he must have got on to something. Mr. Fisher then explained the extraordinarily involved lives of himself and his dead wife.

He told us that he and his wife had lived in Twickenham with their two daughters, but, before the outbreak of war, they had become estranged and, without seriously thinking of parting, each had taken a lover. Mrs. Fisher had met the Dane, and he, Mr. Fisher, had become enamoured of a young widow called Florence Iris Ouida Ransom, whom he called Julia. Both the Dane and Mrs. Ransom went frequently to the house at Twickenham and the Fisher *ménage* remained comparatively tranquil. Then Fisher took " Crittenden," the cottage at Matfield, and spent weekends there with his Julia. By the time war began, the elder Miss Fisher had married and left Twickenham and, in October, 1939, the home broke up. Fisher went to the farm near Bicester, and soon afterwards Mrs. Fisher with Freda, who was nineteen, went to the cottage at Matfield. Miss Saunders joined them as housekeeper. Despite this, Fisher said, they all remained on friendly terms and he often went to Matfield to see his wife and daughter.

I looked across at Tansill and saw a satisfied gleam in his eye. His hunch had come off and in that ninety-mile drive we had got some interesting and possibly valuable information. When we arrived at two o'clock the police station was swarming with newspaper-men.

I have many good friends among the Fleet Street crime reporters, who have an uncanny knack of being at the right spot at the right time, so far as they are concerned, but it is frequently the most embarrassing time for the investigator. This was one such occasion, for I wanted nothing to leak out at this delicate stage.

I went in to see the Chief Constable, who told me I was to be in complete charge of the investigation, and after hearing a little more of the facts of the case I went to the scene of the crime at Matfield, some seven miles away. For the first time I had a chance to talk to Tansill alone.

" Well done, Bert," I said. " Did she say anything? "

" No, but she and Fisher seem to have been together for some time."

" What did you think of Mrs. Ransom? "

" A good-looker but tough. Her eyes are a bit queer— sort of vacant."

At the cottage I saw the body of Charlotte Saunders lying on the path at the side of the house. You will remember that it was thought that she had been bludgeoned about the head. I made a quick examination and satisfied myself that she did not die that way, but had in fact been shot in the head with a sporting gun.

About two hundred yards away, in one corner of the orchard, I saw the body of Freda, who had gunshot wounds in the back, and a hundred yards away, in the opposite corner of the orchard, partly in a ditch, was the body of the third woman, Mrs. Fisher. She too had shotgun wounds in the back. Both women were wearing gum-boots. From a quick examination I was satisfied that the cause of death in all three cases was precisely the same. They had all died from gunshot wounds, and my thoughts began to turn to the conversation I had recently had with the servant at Bicester. The phrase he used stuck in my memory: " *Mrs. Fisher had been learning to use a shotgun owned by the cowman.*"

Sergeant Tansill also remembered what I had said. "Looks like the red-haired lady learned quickly," he commented.

I decided that it was essential to have the leading pathologist on this case, so I rang the Yard and asked for Sir Bernard Spilsbury to be called in. Later, I was told that he would come but would not be free until noon on the following day. I did not mind this, because I had plenty to do, and I took a statement from Mr. Fisher, who had, meanwhile, identified the bodies at the mortuary.

In all murder cases it is essential to take statements with extreme caution, and I was ultra-careful about his. It took me several hours, and finally he left the station about 9.30 p.m., I thought for Bicester.

In his statement Mr. Fisher amplified what he had told us, that he was living apart from his wife but was still on visiting terms, as was his daughter. She had in fact only recently spent a holiday at the farm. Both he and his wife knew of the other's extra-marital association, and neither raised any objections.

I had previously made an examination of the cottage while Sergeant Tansill carried on with the statement. The rooms were in great disorder. Jewellery, money and other valuables were strewn all over the rooms, and also in a wooden house in the gardens which had been used by Miss Saunders. It seemed that the murderer had intended it to appear that robbery was the motive for the crime. In the kitchen on the floor was a tea-tray and a quantity of broken crockery. I had this collected and pieced together. The result was that there were in fact four cups, four saucers, four plates, in fact four of everything. *Four people.* . . .

This suggested that Miss Saunders was in the act of preparing tea for four persons and had come face to face with the person who was going to murder her. The question was—who was the fourth person? My construction of the case at that time was that someone well known to the deceased women had arrived at the cottage that afternoon with a shotgun, and, as Mrs. Fisher and her daughter were wearing gum-boots when found, it could be presumed that they went into the orchard with this person to shoot rabbits, or to shoot at something. The murderer, having got the Fishers into the orchard, and at a reasonable distance from the cottage, first shot the daughter in the back; the mother, seeing what was happening and realising her own danger, ran to the other side of the orchard which was up a slight hill. The murderer followed her, reloading the gun, and shot her in the back.

For the murderer there still remained the question of Miss Saunders, and she also had to be disposed of. So, returning to the cottage, Miss Saunders might have come face to face with her killer in the kitchen at the rear of the house. I imagined that something in the appearance of the murderer alarmed Miss Saunders who dropped the tray of crockery and ran through the cottage and out of the front door. In my opinion she had intended to run to the main road for help, but, as she passed the end of the cottage, she again saw the murderer, who, guessing her intention, had run round from the back door to intercept her. It was when they met on the corner that Miss Saunders was shot.

There was another strange coincidence. A bicycle, a lady's bicycle, was found in the ditch on the main road only a short distance from the cottage entrance. It was slightly damaged, and the bicycle was identified as one belonging to Mrs. Fisher.

In the orchard between the bodies of Mrs. Fisher and her daughter a lady's white hogskin glove was found. This was a wonderful discovery, because I knew that, if I could find the hand that fitted that glove, I was fairly certain of having found the murderer—or, as I was now almost certain, the murderess.

While this was happening, of course, I sought the assistance of the Yard fingerprint chief, Superintendent Fred Cherrill, and Sergeant Percy Law, now Superintendent, of the Photographic Branch. These officers worked at the cottage until dusk, Cherrill finding the prints and Law photographing them, and then I decided to quit for the day. We adjourned to our hotel for a much-wanted meal and a drink.

The meal over, Sergeant Tansill and I were sitting discussing the events of the day and checking on various statements, while Mr. Cherrill and the others, including Jack Frost, were playing darts. It was a warm evening and Mr. Cherrill was playing in his shirt-sleeves. He always wore a white shirt, and the younger officers were, of course, calling him " Guv'nor." While the game was going on, a resident of the hotel came into the lounge, watched the play for a short time, no doubt heard the manner in which Mr. Cherrill was being addressed, and was perhaps impressed by his grey hair and stout figure. A little later, when Mr. Cherrill was standing by the dartboard, this man walked over to him and said in a loud voice: " I've just booked a phone call to London; will you please let me know when it comes through? " Cherrill looked surprised: " Why me? " The man replied: " Well, you're the guv'nor, aren't you? "

There was a roar of laughter and Cherrill explained that he was the " guv'nor " of the Fingerprint Branch of Scotland Yard and merely a guest in the pub.

I had asked the local police to make some inquiries, and on Thursday morning a boy of fourteen came to the cottage and told Sergeant Tansill, who was waiting for Sir Bernard Spilsbury, that on the previous Tuesday, July 9, he had been on the road outside the cottage and on three occasions saw a woman acting very suspiciously and peering through the hedge into the orchard. He recalled her wearing blue slacks and a coloured jumper. And he also remembered that her fingernails were bright red, and that she had a shock of red hair. Tansill immediately recalled the time he had seen Mrs. Ransom standing in the door at Bicester in precisely that dress, with the bright red fingernails and red hair.

Several other people were found who had been working in the fields between Matfield and Tonbridge, and they described the woman they had seen walking along the road. There was also a little taxi driver, and the ticket collector at the railway station. They all stated that the woman was carrying a long, narrow-shaped brown-paper parcel under her arm, and the taxi driver and the ticket collector said she had boarded the 4.25 p.m. train for London. All agreed on her description. We had collected all this information in a very short time, and now anxiously awaited the arrival of Sir Bernard Spilsbury. He took one look at the three bodies and confirmed that each of the victims had died from shots fired at very close range from a shotgun. I told him all I knew, and he agreed that the person responsible was undoubtedly well known to the deceased persons, judging from the closeness of the gun when fired at the body. He went further and said that he was certain that the killer fired twice more into Mrs. Fisher's back as she lay dying, and then walked back to where the daughter lay and fired once more into her back. By the time Sir Bernard had finished it was getting late, and in view of the blackout conditions I decided to wait till morning before returning to the farm at Bicester.

At six o'clock next morning, Friday, Sergeant Tansill and I, accompanied by Detective Inspector Smeed and his wife, drove over to interview Mrs. Ransom. I took Mrs. Smeed just in case of emergency. When we arrived at the farm I learned that Mrs. Ransom, or Mrs. Fisher as she was known there, had been driven to Aylesbury railway station by the farmhand I had spoken to on my previous visit, and that she was accompanied by the cowman's wife. This farmhand thought Mrs. Ransom was going to London to see Mr. Fisher, who apparently had not returned to the farm since leaving with us on that Wednesday evening. He had not gone to Bicester as I had expected.

Leaving Sergeant Tansill to get the official statements, I went to Aylesbury to check up. I could not get very far with my inquiries, so I telephoned the Yard to warn them that it was possible that Mrs. Ransom would communicate with Mr. Fisher at his City office, and that, should she do so, Detective Superintendent Bell was to be informed immediately. I did not think it would be long before I heard something interesting, and decided to wait at least an hour at the station. In London, Detective Inspector John Black, one of my officers, was looking after inquiries, and Superintendent Bell told me he would keep me informed of what was happening. Within an hour Inspector Black telephoned me to say that Mrs. Ransom had spoken to Mr. Fisher on the telephone, and that an appointment had been made for them to meet at 1.30 p.m. in London at York Road tube station at the far end of Waterloo Bridge. I told Inspector Black to cover this meeting in the event of my being held up. I dashed back to the farm, picked up my colleagues and drove fast for London. I got to the appointed place early, as

I wanted to arrive before Mr. Fisher, who by that time was more than a little worried.

Just before one-thirty, Inspector Black drove through and signalled that he wished to speak to me. He told me that the appointment had been changed to 4 p.m at the same place. Later that appointment was again changed to a solicitor's office in High Holborn at 6 p.m. I went along to this office, rather wondering what I would be up against. When I entered, Mr. Fisher was there and so was the cowman's wife, but there was no Mrs. Ransom. I was told that she had gone off to do some shopping.

I decided to wait outside with Sergeant Tansill and Mr. Smeed from Kent, and intercept the woman when she returned. I wondered in fact whether she *would* return.

She did arrive very soon afterwards, and I introduced myself. She made out that she did not know me, and indeed had never seen me before. During this little talk I walked her back along the passage where I had intercepted her, towards my car, and when she saw what was in my mind she persisted that she wished to see her friend in an office round the corner. She did not say, you will notice, that it was in fact a solicitor's office. I had to think fast. Should I let her go or take her straight off to the police station? I decided to go with her to this office. I walked in with her, and her solicitor told her that she had nothing to fear and should go with me to Scotland Yard. He also said that he would be on hand if she needed him.

I left with Mr. Fisher, Mrs. Ransom and the maid and we went to Scotland Yard. As we approached my car I noticed a squad of newspaper reporters and photographers. The cameras were clicking merrily, and I recognised one of the reporters. I was annoyed at this stage that photographers were so close on my tracks, because I would very probably be faced with the question of identification. I had certain evidence, but knew perfectly well that the backbone of my case would be to have this woman picked out at an identification parade, and I could not afford to have a picture blazoned across the pages of the national newspapers, which would inevitably prejudice any parade. When I got inside the Yard I reported the fact that photographers had been taking pictures, and asked that the papers be contacted and urged not to use any photographs of this woman since it would hinder my investigation. As always, Fleet Street was happy to work with the C.I.D. and no picture was used until after the identification parade.

Mrs. Ransom, a very attractive, slim, pleasant-spoken woman, was quite talkative. She persisted in her statement that she had not been to Matfield on Tuesday, July 9. She claimed instead that she had been about the farm the whole of that day and asserted that her servants could prove it. Her statement in fact was a complete alibi and took some considerable time to write down. After it was completed and she had signed it, I told her she would be detained and taken to Tonbridge police station, where she would be put up for identification. A statement was next taken from the cowman's wife, who made some remarkable disclosures. She stated that her husband was in fact Mrs. Ransom's brother and that the elderly housekeeper at the farm was Mrs. Ransom's mother. These facts were not known to Mr. Fisher, and you can well imagine his surprise when I told him.

It was now early morning, and I arranged that Mr. Smeed should take Mrs. Ransom to Tonbridge later in the day and I would return to the farm to interview the cowman and the housekeeper. Before Mrs. Ransom was taken away, however, I challenged her with the information concerning her mother and brother. This she strenuously denied.

At the farm the housekeeper and her cowman son were interviewed and admitted their relationship with Mrs. Ransom. The cowman also told us that he had taught Mrs.

Ransom to ride a bicycle and also to fire a shotgun, which, he said, Mrs. Ransom had borrowed from him on the 8th of July and returned on the 10th, saying that it was dirty and wanted cleaning. I needed very little more. It was after midnight when I arrived back in Tonbridge.

On the Monday, just six days after I had begun this investigation, I held an identification parade. I got eight women as much like Mrs. Ransom as possible and all dressed in slacks and jumpers. Mrs. Ransom, too, was similarly dressed. The parade was held and, as I expected, Mrs. Ransom was picked out by several witnesses as having been seen at Tonbridge and Matfield on July 9, 1940.

After the parade was over I invited Mrs. Ransom to try on the glove which had been found in the orchard, and although she disclaimed ownership it fitted her perfectly. I had searched, and had many other policemen search, all the grounds and all Mrs. Ransom's belongings but I could not find the partner to that glove. It could have been, of course, that she had realised the importance of the dropped glove and had disposed of the other one.

I had another thought and asked the local police doctor to examine Mrs. Ransom for any signs of a fall, such as from a bicycle. He discovered a grazing on one knee which he said could be accounted for in that way. I was now chasing up fast. The whole case was opening out and becoming clear.

Inquiries at the railway station at Bicester produced a witness, the stationmaster, who remembered a woman dressed in slacks and carrying a long narrow parcel who boarded the 8.56 a.m. train for London on July 9. That parcel, which you will remember was mentioned earlier by other witnesses, could have been a shotgun folded up. Other inquiries disclosed that Mrs. Ransom could have reached Tonbridge via London at 12.8 p.m., and leaving there by the 4.25 train as stated by the ticket collector, would have reached home about 7 p.m. It was Mrs. Ransom's habit to meet Mr. Fisher as he drove into the farm about 6.30 p.m. each evening, but he did not see her that evening until much later. An excuse for that was that she was unwell.

The evidence against Mrs. Ransom had snowballed and become tremendously powerful. I had no hesitation at all in charging her with all three murders. At the trial at the Old Bailey in November, 1940, the housekeeper and the cowman gave evidence and told of their relationship with the accused, and both agreed that, on July 9, she appeared to be missing from the farm during the day. Mrs. Ransom, who had stood several hours of strenuous questioning in the witness-box, again emphatically denied her relationship to her mother and brother. She was found guilty and sentenced to death; and, after her appeal had failed, was certified insane—which was no part of the defence—and sent to Broadmoor, where she is still.

This is the story of a triple murderess, a widow, an adventuress of many years' standing, who was arrested very soon after the murders were committed and found guilty upon overwhelming circumstantial evidence.

Since then she has become almost famous in Broadmoor as the leading light in the operatic society, and has possibly had more publicity since being there, than she ever had before this case, because she has taken the lead in so many theatrical productions.

CHAPTER SEVEN

THE BARNSLEY MURDER

EARLY IN 1943, again on a Monday morning, assistance was sought from the " Yard," by the then Chief Constable of Barnsley, in Yorkshire, in connection with a brutal attack upon a Land Army girl in a fairground in that town.

At that time it was not known exactly how the attack had occurred, and as there were a large number of troops stationed in and around there it was decided to seek assistance without delay, in order that the officers to be sent would reach Barnsley that evening.

Now Barnsley is a coal mining town, fairly thickly populated, within quite a small radius, and quite a good shopping centre. The Police Force there consisted of some 91 officers and men, and the Chief Constable, Mr. H. T. Williams, had been there all his service, from constable upwards.

Strangely enough at this particular period, early May, 1943, there were already four " Yard " officers in two other places in Yorkshire investigating murders, namely, Detective Chief Inspector Greeno and his Sergeant, and Detective Chief Inspector Thorp and his Sergeant, at Halifax and Scarborough, respectively.

As you will have guessed I was detailed for the Barnsley inquiry, and with Detective Sergeant Webb, I left King's Cross at about 1 p.m., bound for the North.

Once again, of course, there was no food on the crowded train, since we were living under strict wartime conditions, and we had foolishly forgotten to get ourselves any sandwiches in advance, so that we were starving when we arrived at Barnsley after a tortuous slow train journey from Doncaster, where we had to change. We were driven direct to the police station to meet the Chief Constable, who soon made us feel at home, and Detective Inspector Harrison.

We learned that the girl had died while we had been travelling. Inspector Harrison told us that, when the Yard's assistance was sought, the girl had not yet been identified. Since then, the local police had discovered that her name was Violet Wakefield, aged twenty, and she lived in a small village called Cudworth, some five miles outside Barnsley. She was working in the Land Army, living at home, and each morning left shortly after seven o'clock to go by bus to Barnsley, where she changed to another bus to get to a village named Porthorn, where she worked on a farm. This village was on the opposite side of Barnsley to Cudworth. A number of witnesses had established that she had left home as usual on that morning, and other people said that when she left the bus at Barnsley she was met by a young man. The couple were seen to walk off together towards the place where she would have to pick up the second bus. That direction was also the way to the fairground. Some time later the young man had been seen walking alone from the fairground.

Once the girl's identity had been established, the police soon found out that she was engaged to a local young man named Trevor Elvin, who was twenty-one, and had been missing from his home since about eight o'clock that morning. It seemed that a good many people had seen the couple together that morning.

First I decided to see the body, which was lying in the local mortuary.

She had been a pretty girl, and it was clear that she had died from severe wounds on the head. After that I went to the fairground and examined the spot inside the " Dodgem " car tent where she had been found. I made a thorough search of the ground, and this showed definite signs of a struggle, with much blood spattered around. Some grass had been beaten down and there were marks in the soft earth, as this fight—which perhaps lasted only a few seconds—had gone on and ended in death.

I was handed a rusty old hammer which had been found near the body, and I met the unblinking eyes of Sergeant Webb. " This looks like the weapon, guv'nor," he said. " And those spots look like blood spots." I was inclined to agree with him. The striking end of the hammer was missing, leaving only the curved sharp piece on the other side. It looked as though the striking end had been broken off some time before, as the break was quite rusty. It looked rather like the sort of hammer that had been used in the house for breaking coals and general odd jobs.

There were no more clues to be found at the actual scene, so I decided to visit the home of this young man, Trevor Elvin. He was still out, but I saw his mother, a pleasant woman, and very distressed at the disappearance of her son. I also saw an uncle of the young man, and both he and Mrs. Elvin understood how grave the situation looked, but they were most helpful. They asked me into their home, a typical small country home, very neat and tidy, with the smell of fresh baking, and garden flowers standing in vases round the room. Mrs. Elvin said that her husband was in the Forces, and then she told me about her boy.

He was apparently on the sick list and so not attending his employment as an engineer. That morning he left home about seven-thirty, saying he was going to see Violet, whom they knew, and she said that he was then wearing his raincoat. Mrs. Elvin was working part time in a local shop to help make ends meet, and she left home just before eight o'clock each morning. She distinctly remembered her son returning just before that time carrying his raincoat over his arm. She spoke to him, but he did not reply; and then he went to another part of the house, came back into the living-room almost immediately and left the house—this time without his raincoat. I said to her: " Mrs. Elvin, do you have any idea where your son would be likely to go ? " She said: " I can't think where he would go at this time. It is most unusual and I'm terribly worried."

The raincoat was in the house and I took possession of it. I also found out from the mother that there had been a similar hammer to that found at the fairground kept in the house and used for breaking coals. I wondered if the missing head would by any chance still be in the house, and asked Mrs. Elvin if we might search. She agreed at once, and we went straight to the cellar. At one end was a pile of coals and near the wall a large junk-box full of old nuts and bolts, screwdrivers, lengths of wire, pieces of rope. Right at the very bottom was the missing part of the hammer, and clearly it had been there some time. The break in the steel was still quite distinct although rather less rusty than the part which we had found at the scene of the crime. I took possession of the head of the hammer and left the house.

While Sergeant Webb completed the statements at the house from Mrs. Elvin and the uncle, I went to the local station and sent a message to all police forces near where her relatives lived ordering inquiries to be made, and asking urgently if this young man had been seen. Before long the police at Otley in Yorkshire came on the phone to say that Trevor Elvin had been there earlier and borrowed some money. About two hours later, the Blackpool police phoned to say the boy had been found at the home of an uncle of his, and was reported to be suffering from loss of memory. I asked the police there to take him to the nearest station, detain and search him.

Many hours had gone by since we had arrived there and we had still had no food. Equally, I was most anxious to get to Blackpool, and in view of the blackout conditions

Chief Superintendent Beveridge politely raises his hat as he arrests Mrs. Florence Ransom in High Holborn

A group picture taken at the retirement in 1945 of Sir Norman Kendal, the Assistant Commissioner C.I.D., seen centre front with his Detective Superintendents and other senior officers. *Front row* (left to right): Detective Supt. P. Worth, Ronald Howe, Deputy Assistant Commissioner, Sir Norman Kendal, Assistant Commissioner, H. Young, Chief Constable C.I.D., and Detective Supt. F. Cherrill. *Back row* (left to right): Detective Supt. G. Hatherill, Detective Supt. W. Parker, Detective Supt. T. Thompson, travelling was slow and difficult. After some discussion it was decided that it would be best to go by road and arrive in Blackpool around six in the morning. With reasonable luck we would then be back in Barnsley for lunch, and in time for the post-mortem which was to be held at 2 p.m. I would point out here that it is always necessary for the investigating officer in charge of the case to be present at the post-mortem.

We set out in a police car—Inspector Harrison, Sergeant Webb, a driver and myself—and after losing our way several times, as there were no signposts and we were inexpert map readers, we arrived at Blackpool shortly after 6 a.m. I met the Chief Constable, Mr. Harry Barnes, who is still there today, and he allowed us to see Elvin. Before we went in, he showed me some letters which had been taken from Elvin's pockets. He had written them to relatives apologising for what had happened and asking forgiveness. Elvin was brought in, and it was immediately clear to me that he was feigning loss of memory.

" Is your name Trevor Elvin? " I asked.

" Yes."

" I am Chief Inspector Beveridge from Scotland Yard, and I am making inquiries into the death of Miss Violet Wakefield. Can you tell me where you were yesterday morning? " Elvin looked quite blank and said: " I can't remember anything." I could see that he had decided to say nothing and to continue to act his part. I wasted no more time with him, and had a hurried breakfast. Then we left again for Barnsley, taking Trevor Elvin with us.

At the police station at Barnsley I could not stop him talking and in the C.I.D. office he made a long written statement which Sergeant Webb wrote down. He referred to his jealousy of a man working on the same farm as Violet, and of the quarrel they had had on the previous evening. He spoke of getting up to meet her in the morning and of taking the hammer with him, which he said he took merely to frighten her. He clearly remembered meeting her as she came off the bus and walking along the street towards the fairground but said he could recall nothing more.

The fact that he did not tell me everything mattered little, for, with those letters, his own confession of having met the girl shortly before she was killed, the finding of the missing part of the hammer in his house and the statements of witnesses, the case was pretty well tied up. For the first time since we arrived from London, Webb and I went to our hotel, which had been booked while we were travelling. We met the proprietor, Angus Seed, brother of the famous Jimmy Seed, then manager of Charlton Athletic football club in London. He told us that when he saw our beds had not been slept in he had accused the night porter of going to sleep and not hearing us at the door. We were able to exonerate the porter, explaining that we had worked all night.

The post-mortem examination revealed that the dead girl had extensive head injuries consistent with having been caused by the hammer we had found. All the witnesses had now been seen, and statements taken from them, and it was clear from our inquiries that there was no foundation for Elvin's jealousy and, indeed, all the evidence proved that his victim was a young woman of the greatest integrity.

At his trial at Leeds Assizes, Elvin pleaded insanity. His defence suggested that he had suffered from schizophrenia (split mind), but there was no evidence to support it and he was found guilty and sentenced to death. His appeal failed, and he was executed at Leeds Gaol for a violent and quite unnecessary crime.

CHAPTER EIGHT

THE FLYING SQUAD

WHEN I RETURNED to the Squad office a few months later, the crime situation was worse. In my absence, the country housebreakers had been cleaned up following information that there were a number of men and women employed in the West End whose sole job was to spot wealthy people away from home, and then pass on the information to their leaders. London was having its greatest trial, for German bombs were falling everywhere, with looters constantly on the prowl. Hardly a night went by without all my Squad men being out on duty, sometimes helping to rescue injured people, and often arresting looters. Many a looter got away from my detectives merely because they were too busy helping to save lives. On one occasion I saw practically the entire Flying Squad working like beavers tearing away rubble from a badly bombed house in Bloomsbury in which many people were trapped. This was not strictly part of their job, for there were plenty of rescue workers around, but there was no stopping them.

A night rarely went by without one of the cars being involved in a hectic chase. One night a call came from Bond Street about a suspect car, and it was relayed to a Squad car which was then in Regent Street. The driver accelerated through the side streets and recognised the car by description. It was then standing outside a jeweller's shop window. As the Squad car drove up two masked men were walking towards the window, one carrying a hammer and the other a truncheon. There was a look-out man and a fourth at the wheel of the bandit car with its engine running. The look-out man saw the Squad car, shouted a warning, and they jumped in and shot away. The Squad car chased through the West End, through Hyde Park, down to Victoria, doubled back to Westminster, through more side streets, and finally near the Houses of Parliament the Squad car got in front and edged the bandits into the kerb. There was a fierce fight with no quarter, and at the end three of the men were arrested. The fourth was picked up a little later.

When that car was searched my detectives found masks, jemmies, truncheons and grappling hooks—this last something we had not come across before. It was found later that they were used to hook on to the grilles of jewellers' shops and then the car was driven a few yards, pulling the grilles away from the window and leaving the property at the mercy of the thieves.

Don't think, for a second, that every Squad job was as exciting and dramatic. Some of the biggest began from almost nothing. In one case a man was found in possession of a cash-box containing £15. He was unable to explain where he got it, and that cash-box was later identified as the proceeds of a housebreaking in Highgate. That was a small enough beginning, but more inquiries revealed that this same man had broken into twelve other houses in the area.

Over the radio one day in January, 1941, a message came which said briefly: " Wanted: Bernard Silver escaped today from a working party at Pentonville Prison." That was all. A quick phone call by the chief to the car nearest to Pentonville elicited the information that Silver had jumped on a bus outside the prison in busy Caledonian Road and disappeared. It was also known that he was desperately anxious to see his wife for some reason, and only three hours later an informant was on the phone to the Yard to say that Silver had a rendezvous with his wife at Tottenham Court Road underground station. He arrived, as did his wife, and also two Squad men.

The thieves missed very few tricks at a time when practically every commodity was controlled by coupons. They decided to make a corner in clothing and petrol coupons and ration cards, and they very nearly succeeded. Their depredations were such that one day I was called in by Sir Norman Kendal, the Assistant Commissioner for Crime, who told me that the Squad must stop these offences because they were threatening the whole ration scheme of the country.

Merchants delivered all their clothing coupons to the local Food Office, and here we found the first big snag. So many envelopes of coupons came in that the civil servants were forced to accept them on trust. The merchants wrote on the outside the number of coupons the envelopes contained, but frequently when the envelopes were examined they were found to be full of plain paper. The thieves did not stop there. They stole enormous quantities of sweet coupons, and thefts of petrol coupons and ration books later became almost as big a menace. So many people had access to these coupons that it was difficult to catch the men behind the racket. We did, however, manage to net hundreds of small fry, and gradually began to get a stranglehold on the big operators, and arrested one after the other. We were aided by brilliant observation from some of our own men and equally useful information passed on to us by our informants.

Even the big business men were not proof against the cunning of some of these thieves. Some of them were duped by the story that, if they went to a certain house, they could purchase a large quantity of some precious commodity like syrup or sugar. One man, whose name is now a household word, went to a house on the outskirts of London and took with him £1,200 in cash for a load of whisky. As soon as he walked into the house he was bound and gagged and his money taken from him. That was a case which should never have happened, and I had little sympathy for the victim. We did get the thieves on that occasion and they were all given long sentences.

It is possible to form a fair idea of the volume of crime in those days when I say that during my time with the Flying Squad black marketeers were fined a total of £11,000. Each year crime grew slightly worse until the number of arrests increased. In 1940 we made 663 arrests; in 1941 that figure rose to 767. In 1942 it rose again to 862 arrests. And with those arrests, mostly of thieves, there were many receivers, who are the hardest people in the world to catch. One of the reasons is that the law states that they must have *knowingly* received stolen property, which is a state of mind and therefore difficult to prove. The other point in favour of receivers is that the thief will rarely give away the identity of the man who buys his stolen goods. If he has no receiver, he cannot work so easily.

By early 1942, the deserters had also become organised. They bought identity cards and few of them needed ration books since they all ate in cafés. There were Poles, Czechs, French-Canadians, who joined up with the British and pillaged wherever they could. I discovered that there were in fact four gangs each living in a separate corner of London. With the menace of these deserters came something even more important. We discovered that some of them were using guns, which at that time were easy to obtain.

One night, at a West End restaurant, a man had been refused admission. The doorman asked him to leave, and was then faced with a gun. He aimed a terrific blow at the gunman, who ducked and ran away, and a message went out over the air to my cars. They found the man who, when challenged, drew his gun, but a Flying Squad sergeant flung himself at the man's feet and pulled him over, and in a second he was tight in the embrace—none too tender—of three more detectives. I am happy to say that he drew two years' hard labour.

At about the same time, rumours began to reach me of a conspiracy to dope greyhounds at various tracks up and down the country. At last, after several months of probing, we found a lead to this, and it turned into the first dog-doping prosecution ever known in London. It began on June 1, 1942, and lasted for several weeks, during which a team of my men had to keep many hundreds of hours of observation. We had discovered that the idea of this gang was to dope and thereby incapacitate possibly three dogs in one race, which meant that the first and second must be found in the other three. By wagering large sums of money on the remaining three it was possible to bring off a very useful coup.

This particular story began in a rather luxurious club in the West End, where an attractive young woman with a considerable knowledge of dogs was engaged in conversation by a man. Over several drinks he found out that the young woman was unemployed, and suggested that he could find her an interesting job, possibly in the kennels at Wembley Stadium. Such a position had already been advertised. When he had gained her confidence he told her part of the truth, which was that he was a representative of a dog-doping syndicate, and that she could make herself a great deal of money in the position of kennelmaid, able to administer the drugs.

This was a big temptation to anyone, particularly as in this case the woman was unemployed and short of funds. The temptation became even greater when, two days later, a second man visited her flat and explained that he had been given her name and address and understood that she was interested in a vacancy as kennelmaid at Wembley. She assured him that she wanted the job. He was delighted with her enthusiasm and talked about his plans for the successful doping of greyhounds. He told her that if she was successful in getting the Wembley job he would pay her £50 at once, but he would leave her there for at least three weeks so that she could get used to the dogs before starting to work on them. He proposed to dope the dogs with pills, which he explained was very simple, and promised her £400 the first time she used them.

This man made the mistake of talking too much too soon, for he frightened the young woman who, after she had talked the whole matter over with a friend, decided to go to the police.

Detective Inspector John Ball and Detective Sergeant John Gosling (both now superintendents) took charge of the job and saw the young woman. After a talk with her they telephoned me and I suggested that she should henceforth act on police instructions. She agreed, and a further appointment was arranged.

I decided that it was necessary to mention the whole matter to the Wembley Stadium authorities, and contacted their security officer, ex-Detective Chief Inspector Hector McPherson. He arranged an appointment for me with Sir Arthur Elvin who, after I had explained the situation, readily agreed to co-operate. Accordingly the young woman, who by this time had applied for the job of kennelmaid, was interviewed by an unsuspecting staff manager and given the job. It was fortunate that she had the necessary qualifications and therefore had got the job on her own merits.

The young woman continued to meet the second man, and each meeting was closely observed by Inspector Ball and Sergeants Gosling and Veasey. Whenever possible after the meeting, she came secretly to the Squad office at the Yard and made a statement.

One day this man failed to keep an appointment with her, and she was unable to contact him at any of his usual haunts. I wondered if he had realised what was happening. For a few days we feared that our plans had gone awry, but suddenly the woman telephoned to say that she had heard from the man, who was sending her some money. Apparently he had telephoned from Scotland, and in the next few days she had several other phone calls, but, most important of all, she received two money orders. That was important evidence as far as we were concerned.

Eventually the man did return to London and immediately resumed contact with the woman who was working for us. At one of these meetings she was introduced to a third man who, like the other two, questioned her at some length. She didn't like him—he seemed to be much more cunning than the others and had a great deal more to say.

Several other appointments were made between the men and this woman, but each time the men failed to appear. When later she spoke to them about this they laughed and said they were playing safe, testing her out to see if she was playing straight with them. But eventually she seemed to satisfy them and they invited her to their flat for further discussions. It was there she met the fourth member, a woman, who from then on took an active part in the whole conspiracy.

The plot now began to get going. It was explained to the young woman that capsules would be given to the animal four hours before a race, and that when this was done she was to let one of the syndicate know that all was well, and they would then back the remaining dogs. It was agreed that she would be paid £25 a week for the first few weeks, and subsequently £300 or £400 whenever she administered dope, according to the winnings. Once she was shown a box of capsules which were alleged to be the actual dope, but she was not allowed to handle them or to examine the box.

We were slowly getting to the point when we could make an arrest, but there was more to be done. My officers kept observation at one appointment made with the woman at a famous West End hotel, where one of the men handed her a small package wrapped in brown paper. They walked from the hotel into Hyde Park. After a quarter of an hour they returned to the hotel, and the man told her that he was testing her out and asked for the return of the package, telling her there was nothing in it anyway. She returned the package, indignantly demanded an explanation and threatened to withdraw from the whole affair. The man explained that he did this just in case the police were watching because, if they had seen him pass the package, they would be sure to step in and arrest him. It was fortunate for us that my detectives were too well experienced to do anything but watch at this stage.

She seemed now to have completely gained their confidence, and next time she met one of the men who gave her two capsules and told her that they were to be administered to a certain dog running at Wembley the following night. He wanted her to do this to test the reaction of the capsules. She realised, of course, that it was a further test for her and played her part accordingly. The capsules were handed to my detectives the same evening, and I made arrangements with the Wembley authorities that this particular dog should be withdrawn from the race at the last moment, thereby suggesting to the conspirators that the dope had taken effect.

After that race meeting the conspirators met and seemed generally satisfied. They made another appointment for the woman to attend their flat the following evening to be paid. We were watching outside, and as the woman left the flat she gave a pre-arranged signal indicating that all four crooks were in the flat, which was on the fourth floor of a large block in the West End. We rang the bell and were admitted immediately, much to the surprise of the gang. We had in our possession warrants which we read in dead silence. The charge was an unusual one: " Between the 1st of June and the 4th of July 1942 did unlawfully conspire combine confederate and agree to cheat and defraud such persons as might wager sums of money upon the results of greyhound racing at Wembley Stadium by administering a drug to greyhounds competing in such races and thereby influencing the results of the same to the advantage of themselves. Against the peace."

We searched the flat and several boxes of capsules were found. When analysed they were found to contain sixteen grains of Corytone, which is a hypnotic and acts on the nervous system. Later, those four conspirators appeared at the Old Bailey; the three men were sentenced and the woman acquitted. The judge, who was impressed by the way Inspector Ball and Sergeants Gosling and Veasey had handled this case, gave them a strong commendation.

Before leaving the subject of the Flying Squad I must mention my belief that there is little honour among thieves. It is amazing how many informants are used by the police. They do this of course for money, although some of them think, quite wrongly, that if they keep on the right side of the police they will be allowed to carry on their own activities without fear of interruption. Informants are paid through a special Information Fund, but the amount is seldom very large. On the other hand, insurance companies sometimes offer a reward for the recovery of stolen property.

One of the extraordinary things is how these informants manage to survive; it is true that occasionally one will be found with a razor slash on his face, or in some dark alley,

badly knocked about, but I can never remember any of
them being killed, which is a frequent suggestion made in
films.

These men, and sometimes women, find their information
in a variety of ways. They may manage to get the confidence
of criminals who love to boast of their exploits, to talk of
where they have been and how they have been spending
their money. And when they talk, often unwisely, a little
stool-pigeon can quickly run to the telephone and call his
favourite Yard contact. But it is not every officer who can
handle an informer, and indeed some detectives have used
very few throughout their service. There is always the
danger of the bogus informer to be guarded against.

My favourite story of the thief who could not refrain
from boasting concerns a man called Augustus who was so
proud of his exploits that, one night in an East End pub, he
told the assembled company that, when he had been burg-
ling a certain house, which he very kindly named, he had
surprised a dear old lady and had had to lock her in the
bathroom. This sally was greeted with great guffaws by his
cronies but, before he had managed to get another drink,
two of my men had walked into the pub and " claimed "
him. An informant had listened in.

By the summer of 1944, while there was still plenty of
crime for the Flying Squad to investigate, there was also a
feeling of optimism in the air due to the landings in France
on D-Day and continued advances by the Allied troops.
We had been through the V.1 bombardment and that had
diminished a little, and I was beginning to think about taking
my family up to Scotland for a well-earned holiday. But,
as has happened on so many occasions, the holiday had to
be postponed, for early in August I was called to Bedford-
shire to assist in yet another murder investigation.

I remember being in an extremely disgruntled mood
driving down in the hot sunshine through the quiet English

countryside, and wishing selfishly that it had not been my turn. I made my headquarters at a pretty, rose-covered village police station, nearby a place called Kempston Ballast Hole, where a body had been found. This station, which smelt of the country and old books, had never before been the headquarters of a murder probe. On that occasion I had with me Detective Sergeant Herbert Hannam, and soon after we arrived we were met by the local detective inspector, who told us of the murder. It had taken place apparently several days before, and the body had been found lying among some bushes in this ballast hole. Due to the weather, the body was seriously decomposed and had been found by a retired police constable who had been taking his dog for a walk. The local police surgeon had examined it and found serious fractures to the skull.

Soon after my arrival I telephoned for Dr. Keith Simpson, who came down with his secretary. I took them along to the scene of the crime, which was only a short distance from the police station. On the way I told Dr. Simpson that the body was badly decomposed and there might be some difficulty in identifying it. " The teeth may help us there," he commented. I had already come to a similar conclusion and a group of my officers were searching.

Kempston Ballast Hole was a scruffy piece of waste land among old railway sidings with crumbled sleepers and derelict trucks. I conducted the party along the railway track and finally stepped into a patch of tangled grass and bushes with an occasional patch of bright-coloured wild flowers. There was a great mass of derelict tins, broken baths, bits of bicycles, and one or two old buckets.

The body had been found in a particularly dense thicket of elder bushes which had concealed it for some days. I searched all along through the tangled grass for possible clues. There were fragments of old newspapers, dated well before the estimated time of the murder, but about twenty feet from where the body had been hidden the torn-up photograph of a girl and the loop of a man's trouser brace were found.

Despite the hot sun, my sergeant and I searched practically the entire afternoon, but could find nothing else likely to help us. We went back to the mortuary.

This was so old and ill equipped that Dr. Simpson decided to have the body removed to Guy's Hospital where he could examine it properly. I went back to the pretty police station with Sergeant Hannam. Laid out on the lawn, with a background of beautiful rambling roses, were the clothes which had been removed from the body. With Dr. Simpson I squatted down and began to examine them in detail.

I already knew from Dr. Simpson that the assault must have taken place about fourteen days before. This he had judged by the decomposition, the hot weather and the exposed way in which the body had been lying. The clothing of the dead man showed clearly that his body had been dragged to its hiding place under the bushes. The seat of the trousers had been pulled away from the rear brace attachment as though the body had been hauled by the arms or shoulders, the feet trailing on the ground. This tied up with the brace attachment which we had found earlier that afternoon at the ballast hole. Beside the trousers lay a crumpled sports shirt and some socks, but the shoes were missing.

The following day my men had been searching among the grass and bushes at the ballast hole. Nothing turned up there, but the torn picture we had found at the scene proved fruitful. A woman employed at the police station saw the photograph and recognised it as that of a girl who went frequently to a local dance hall. Detectives went there and found the girl, who was shown the dead man's clothes. She was certain they belonged to her cousin Robert Smith, a young man of twenty-two, who had been working for a firewood merchant named Gribble. The girl said she had not seen her cousin since August 6, and she imagined he had given up the firewood round and gone harvesting. She added that Smith had been friendly with Gribble, his employer, and particularly friendly with Kenneth the son, a boy of sixteen.

I went round to Gribble's house with Sergeant Hannam, and Kenneth Gribble was reasonably helpful and appeared to be sincere. He said he had last seen Robert Smith on the afternoon of August 6, when he had paid him his wages in a field about midday. I asked Gribble about the ballast hole and he said he knew the place well, but had never been there at any time with Smith, and not at all during the last six months.

I did not altogether believe him and so I interviewed another youth, a friend of his, who said he had heard Gribble and Smith making an arrangement to meet at the Kempston Ballast Hole at three o'clock on Sunday afternoon, August 6. This youth also said that Gribble and Smith had had a row about money paid to Smith by Kenneth's father.

I went to see Kenneth Gribble again and asked him why he had not told me that he had been to the ballast hole with Smith. " Oh, yes," he said. " I had a date to meet Bob at the ballast hole that Sunday afternoon, but I forgot to mention it to you at the time." I told him I would like to hear about that meeting, and he replied: " Well, there wasn't an actual meeting. I went to the ballast hole at three o'clock to meet Bob, as arranged, but he didn't turn up, and after waiting around for about ten minutes I decided to go home." He added that he had not seen Bob Smith all that afternoon, and not since.

I left Gribble for the time being; he had not made a very good impression upon me. I continued to make some inquiries locally and learned that the caretaker of a little church opposite the public entrance to the ballast hole had taken to the local police station a bicycle which he had found against the church wall on the afternoon of August 6. He had seen it at half-past three that Sunday, and it was still there at midday next day. So he took it to the police station. That bicycle was identified as belonging to Robert Smith.

This was a helpful new lead, and I took the bicycle along to Kenneth Gribble and showed it to him. He said he did not recognise it as Bob's bike. Again I left him. Back at the station I told Sergeant Hannam to get every man he could find and search the ground at the ballast hole, inch by inch. I was certain by this time that somewhere in that tangled mass of grass and shrubs was the murder weapon, possibly a heavy piece of wood, perhaps a club.

By that time I had Dr. Simpson's report, which suggested that such a weapon had been used. In his opinion, Smith had been killed and dragged along the ground to the bushes where he had been concealed. He had not been involved in much of a fight, although he had been a sturdy young man, well able to defend himself. His hands did not suggest that he had done any fighting. Dr. Simpson thought that Smith had been attacked from in front while standing upright, and struck a violent blow from some blunt heavy instrument to the left side of his face. Then he had been hit again in the mouth and eight teeth knocked out. On Smith's left arm were signs of injury which suggested that he had tried to ward off these blows. A third blow had hit him on the jaw and knocked him to the ground. Then, while he lay senseless, he had probably received a fourth violent blow which killed him.

The search went on at the ballast hole for a few days, and then in the thickest bushes about a hundred feet from where the body had been found we discovered a heavy sawn-off

P.C. Nathaniel Edgar,
shot dead on duty

Superintendent Beveridge
leaves the house outside
which P.C. Edgar was mur-
dered. With him are Detective Inspectors Stinton and
Deakin. White plank marks
the spot where the victim fell

Sidney Tiffin, wildfowler, who found the torso of Setty in the Essex marshes

ISRAEL	AIRCRAFT	the equipment of the various forces
1	CONVERTED HALIFAX BOMBER	
1	SPITFIRE (8 Spare)	
2	PROCTORS	
4	CONSOL'S	
3	AUSTERS	Rhem - Marne
4	DAKOTAS	
2	M.T.B's	

RADIO EQUIPMENT (GENERAL)
44 WALKIE TALKIES.
 8 CASES EMERGENCY FIRST AID KIT.
20 LEWIS TYPE MACHINE GUNS
12 CASES BANDAGES
 2 LORRY LOADS OF BOOTS
12 CASES OF ANTI-TANK MINES
 6 ANTI TANK GUNS
 9 BREN GUNS WITH HIGH ANGLE TRIPOD FOR USE AGAINST AIRCRAFT
.22 CASES MUSTARD GAS BOMBS

Facsimile of list of aircraft parts and equipment written by Brian Hume

Patient paper work helped Supt. Beveridge in the Setty case

bough. It was blood-stained and with several hairs adhering to it.

I sent it up by car to the police laboratory, and shortly afterwards the scientists reported that the blood-stains were human, and that one of the hairs, which was seven inches long, was a human head hair, while a number of short ones were eyebrow hairs. All these hairs corresponded with samples taken from Smith's body.

In the search at the ballast hole we had found other things. There were Smith's shoes, the right one in a railway truck and the left farther away; his brown jacket was folded and lying under a blackberry bush, and his hat some distance from there. All these clothes were identified as having been worn by Smith on that Sunday afternoon.

With this fresh evidence I went again to see Kenneth Gribble. Now I was even more suspicious, but still with insufficient evidence to act. I decided that this young man should be watched.

The weeks went by, weeks of patient watching and waiting. The high summer departed and was replaced by the advance guard of autumn. The flowers had gone and the lush grass and thick bushes at the ballast hole thinned to reveal more refuse. And, as the weather changed, so did Kenneth Gribble. It seemed that the crime fascinated him and he talked about it far more than was healthy for a young man of his age. Even more remarkable, he seemed to know more about it than anyone except Sergeant Hannam and myself. On September 20, more than a month after I had called, I decided once again to see young Mr. Gribble. I sent for him at about eight o'clock in the evening and my request apparently caused some consternation. The whole family was upset, the women cried, the men were bewildered, and Kenneth Gribble plainly apprehensive.

In the station, I addressed myself to the young man, using

my sternest tone. " I have reason to believe you know more about the murder of Robert Smith than you have told me, Gribble. Would you like to say anything further ? "

He began to blush, saying he knew nothing more. He persisted in his story, so I sent for his father. When he walked into the room, he looked a broken man and begged his son to tell the truth. The boy began to cry.

" Yes, I did meet Bob Smith at the ballast hole. He threw a piece of tree at me and I hit him with it."

I could see that at last I was to get the truth, and cautioned him. Then he told me that he and Smith had gone to the ballast hole for a rest, and Gribble had said: " You needn't come to work any more. You know you've been doing me out of money on the round." (He was referring to the firewood round.) That started the quarrel and they began to fight. " Smith picked up a piece of wood and threw it at me. I dodged, picked it up and hit him with it. I hit him on the side of the face and he hit me in the stomach. I hit him again on the head and then twice more. He fell down and I hit him twice more on the head. Then I threw away the piece of wood into some bushes because I could see there was blood on it."

That was the story of the killing. He went on to say he had dragged the body into the bushes and seen a photograph out of Smith's pocket. " I tore it up and threw it away," he said. He had discarded Smith's clothes where we had found them and—one thing I did not know—he had burned Smith's wallet.

Gribble was charged with murder and appeared at Leicester Assizes. The case was reduced to manslaughter, the court taking the view that there had been a fight.

It had been a weary job, entirely without glamour and with little publicity owing to the momentous war news of the time, the patching together of tiny clues, much patient waiting, and finally success. I was more than ever delighted to get back to the Flying Squad, which had been functioning merrily in my absence.

*   *   *

Any of my colleagues, particularly the juniors, will tell you that I was never at my best first thing on Monday mornings, which was probably due to having spent an enjoyable Sunday at home and being reluctant to shake off the mantle of leisure. On one particular Monday morning, about the middle of November, 1943, I was in my office dealing with papers and looking at the returns of the previous night's work and the number of arrests, when in walked Commander Hugh Young. I thought he had rather an impish grin on his face, and, without even wishing me good morning, he said: " Have you got your bag packed, Peter? " I realised at once what he meant, but I said: " No, sir, but then I'm not going anywhere." " Oh yes, you are," he smiled. " You're going down to Somerset today on a murder." I heard this news with mixed feelings. I had plenty of interesting Squad work on hand but London with its food and drink shortage was not much fun and the country could not be worse.

Commander Young told me that he had received a request that morning from the Chief Constable of Somerset for assistance in probing a case of suspected child murder. He told me that he had learned some brief details on the telephone, and it appeared that a regular sergeant in the Army and a woman had been detained from the previous day, but that so far the police were unable to find the body. Here was a new situation, for, instead of going on a murder to find the culprits, I was going to find the victim, with the possible culprits already in custody.

There were a good many sergeants who would have liked to go on the job, for they, too, were tired of wartime

London, but again I chose Albert Webb (now Superintendent) and we set off by train for Yeovil.

We arrived at about 6.30 p.m. and were met by a uniformed constable with a car who drove us to the station, a magnificent new building with every modern appliance and surrounded by a beautifully laid-out garden. We were ushered into an office where sat three healthy-looking officers in uniform, while in a corner was the local detective inspector. I was introduced to the people in the room, and after a brief chat was left with the C.I.D. man, who delighted me by saying: " I have a bottle of Scotch in my room, and I'm sure you're both thirsty." We were not only thirsty but Scotch had practically disappeared, and Yeovil looked a brighter place. Over a drink the inspector talked. He told me that this Army sergeant, a married man with a wife and family in London, was earlier that year stationed at Milborne Port, near Yeovil, and had taken a furnished room near the camp for his wife, who he said was joining him there. The " wife " duly arrived on October 11, 1943, and it was soon apparent to Mrs. Gibbs, the landlady, that she was pregnant; it also soon became obvious to this very homely woman that no preparations had been made for the new arrival, and she was forced to the conclusion that this was an unwanted child.

The child was born on October 21, but meantime the sergeant had been transferred to Witney, in Oxfordshire, where he was an instructor. Mrs. Gibbs understood that other arrangements were going to be made for the woman and her child, and that the sergeant expected to come on leave on November 12 for ten days, when final arrangements would be made for the child to go to the woman's mother in London. The sergeant arrived, and Mrs. Gibbs was later told that the woman's mother was taking the child.

On the morning of the intended trip to London the couple were still in bed at nine o'clock. When they eventually appeared, Mrs. Gibbs noticed that the baby had not been changed. This kindly lady supplied a clean change of clothing and the couple left the house at about 10.45 a.m. to catch the 11.5 train for London. Mrs. Gibbs noticed that the man was then carrying two small cases, whilst the woman carried the baby. The inspector explained that the house occupied by Mrs. Gibbs was in a small terrace on a country road, which led to Milborne Port railway station about a mile away. The road was little used and there was woodland and fields on both sides.

The couple had informed Mrs. Gibbs that they would be back about 9 p.m. but, as they had not returned at 9.30 p.m., she put out the light and retired to bed, leaving the outer street door unlocked Shortly afterwards she heard the outside door open and the couple creep into the house. She confronted them, more out of curiosity than anything else, and noticed that the man was still carrying the two small cases. He told Mrs. Gibbs that they had been to London and had left the baby with the woman's mother. Somehow Mrs. Gibbs, this very honest, good woman, was suspicious. She was not normally given to such thoughts about other people, but she adored children and felt that something had gone wrong. She could not get out of her mind that the baby was unwanted and could not understand why it should be necessary to take two small cases to London and bring them back again.

A day or two later she had further reason for suspicion, for she made a search of their room. She could only see one of the small cases, which she thought was strange, but there was a large case which had been used as a cot for the child. Upon opening this, she saw the second small case inside. More alarming still, she discovered that the change of clothing she had supplied for the child on the morning they had left for London, and several other pieces of its baby garments, were also in the big case alongside the small one, which was locked. Mrs. Gibbs was shocked, as she realised what might have happened.

The following day, Detective Inspector James Dunn drove down and interviewed the woman in Mrs. Gibbs's house and put some searching questions to her regarding the child. She maintained that it was with her mother in London. Inspector Dunn got the mother's address and telephoned the Central Office at the Yard asking for a check to be made. He was given the answer he expected. There was no child. Inspector Dunn then took a statement under caution from the woman, and in it she spoke of her association with the sergeant at Wakefield, since 1940 or 1941 when she lived with him as his wife, and how they eventually went through a form of marriage there earlier in 1943, although she knew perfectly well that he was already a married man.

She spoke of the day they left Mrs. Gibbs's house with the baby for London, and asserted that along the lonely country road they turned off into a lane as they had no intention of going to London. They walked into a wood, where the sergeant asked for the baby. She gave him the child and, taking one of the small cases, he walked on into the woods while she remained there waiting for him. He returned some time later without the baby, but still carrying the case. They went on to Yeovil, where the sergeant deposited the cases in the left luggage office at the railway station, and they had a meal and visited the pictures, to pass the time away until they could return to Mrs. Gibbs's house. The woman said she had asked the sergeant what had happened to the baby, and he told her not to worry. Later that night they returned to Milborne Port with the two cases and waited outside for Mrs. Gibbs to go to bed. Seeing the light extinguished they then crept into the house, as Mrs. Gibbs had said.

The woman insisted that she had no knowledge of what

had happened to the child and, as if to impress this upon the inspector, she said that the sergeant, whose name was Digby, had done the same thing with a previous baby she had had by him some eighteen months earlier somewhere in Kent. Inspector Dunn, of course, detained the woman and went to Witney to interview Digby. There he met a very defiant sergeant, who maintained that the child was with the woman's mother in London, and refused to discuss the matter further. So he was brought to Yeovil and detained, and the following morning assistance was sought from the Yard.

I must mention here that, on the day I was sent to Yeovil, it had been decided by the local police to charge the woman with child abandonment.

Next morning I saw Digby at the local station and told him I had taken over the inquiry and would be seeing him later. Then, with Inspector Dunn and Sergeant Webb, I made a search of the room which had been occupied by Digby and the woman, and there found letters from him which proved there was no doubt of what was intended to happen to that unfortunate child. In some of them there was a reference to a previous child, but in the main the letters hinted that he would find a way of disposing of the child and that she was not to worry.

In view of this, I dispatched Inspector Dunn to Witney to search Digby's belongings there, and at the same time to make what inquiries he could concerning the two small cases. Here again a large number of letters were found from the woman to Digby. She inquired if it was his intention to do the same to this child as he had done to the other one. In addition, Inspector Dunn discovered that Digby had borrowed one of the small cases from another soldier when he went on leave, and that later he had returned it. That man was traced, and the case found and examined. Inside, the inspector found what appeared to be blood-stains, and on examination at the laboratory his first suspicion was proved correct. This also proved the theory that, when Digby left Milborne Port that day to return to Witney, he had the body of the child in the case, as Mrs. Gibbs had suspected. In consequence, the local police, who had been most helpful, agreed to search the very extensive woods surrounding the camp at Witney. Meantime, the police were searching in the woods near Milborne Port, although I was fairly certain that Digby had, in fact, taken the body with him to Witney. But I was taking no chances. We were not helped at this time by the weather. The cold was intense, and I had to wear gum-boots the whole day, so that by evening my legs were so stiff I could hardly walk.

I remember it was a Tuesday evening when I had a brief interview with Digby, and I told him precisely what was happening. He looked me straight in the eye and said: " I don't know what you are talking about. Leave me alone." I was pleased to see that he was a little more shaky. I decided to leave him till the following day, when I would be in possession of all the letters and the blood-stained case.

The following morning, Sergeant Webb and I spent several hours with Digby, who made a long statement concerning his association with the woman, whom he described as being very persistent. He had apparently gone through a form of marriage with her when she discovered she was pregnant. She knew perfectly well, he said, that he was already a married man. His financial position, he said, was very poor, as he was making an allotment to his wife, and therefore could not make one to this other woman. He tried to explain the letters away by saying they were just something to put the woman off, and, as far as the blood-stains were concerned, he simply couldn't account for them at all.

I left him that night, near breaking point, and I was not surprised when on the following morning he sent a message saying he would like to tell me about the whole affair. I sat and listened to this sergeant, now docile, telling his horrifying story of child murder. It made me feel sick.

The position was pretty well what I had imagined. The unwanted baby, and the continual pressure from the woman to find her accommodation, had driven him to despair. He said that when he took the baby into the woods he stumbled and the baby fell to the ground and cut its head. The baby was still alive when he put it in the small case and joined the woman. Later he looked at the baby and saw that it was dead. Digby went on to say that he then left it in the wood whilst he and the woman went to a cinema in Yeovil! Later he returned and found the child still there, so he decided to take it with him to the camp at Witney and bury it in the woods. I suspected that he had not told me everything, but it was enough for the moment.

Mrs. Gibbs had been right in her surmise that when he left Milborne Port to return to Witney the body of the baby was in the case.

Owing to the dense woods around the camp at Witney, I decided to take the suspect with me to point out where he had hidden the body. In the presence of the local police, Inspector Dunn, Sergeant Webb and myself, he unearthed the body of the baby from a rabbit hole. There was a noticeable abrasion on the head. I got the necessary permission to remove the body from one county to another and returned to Yeovil with Digby.

At about midnight on the same day, Professor James Webster, the pathologist, made a post-mortem examination. This revealed that death was due to the injury to the head, and in his opinion consistent with the head having been hit by something hard while resting against the ground. The injuries, he said, could not have been caused by falling from anyone's arms. This was what I had suspected; Digby had decided to tell only part of the truth.

The following day, he and the woman were jointly charged with the murder of the child, and committed for trial to Taunton Assizes. There they were separately represented by counsel, and after several days Digby was found guilty and sentenced to death, and the woman not guilty and acquitted. The customary appeal was dismissed and Digby was duly executed at Bristol Gaol. As far as the second child was concerned, Digby said he had disposed of the body somewhere in Kent, but extensive searches failed to yield any remains.

It appeared that Digby had not confined his amorous activities to only one woman apart from his wife. Inquiries made by the police revealed that he had represented himself as a single man to many other girls at the various places where he had been stationed in England. Even when cohabiting with this woman with whom he was charged, correspondence was passing between him and these various girls, all of whom were seen by us during our inquiries. You can well imagine their shock at our visit. I also had the unpleasant job of interviewing Digby's legal wife. She was a pleasant little woman, and I must say she took the news fairly well.

There is no doubt at all that there would have been no case to investigate had it not been for the suspicions of Mrs. Gibbs, and the fact that she was a good, honest woman and observant. It happens in so many cases that men and women prefer to " mind their own business," and say nothing to the police. But Mrs. Gibbs, fortunately for justice, was interested in knowing what had happened to that child, and passed her suspicions on to the police. Had it not been for that, I am quite certain that the poor unwanted baby would have lain in the woods for months and finally disappeared or been in such a bad condition as to have been unrecognisable and therefore unidentifiable. When, in my experience, one came across a case where the body of the

victim could not be identified, the chances of catching up
with the murderer or murderess were reduced to a very
small percentage.

*   *   *

Back in the Squad office, I found my men busy. The
informants were being helpful. One telephoned to say
that some rings stolen from Kingston were, at that moment,
being melted down before being sold in Hatton Garden.
Fifteen minutes later three men were surprised with their
crucible and Bunsen burner and on their way to Kingston
to be charged with shopbreaking.

Railway thieves were also a constant source of trouble.
It was estimated that they got away with more than
£1,000,000 worth of property every year. Ordinary pilfer-
ing accounted for much of that sum, but the most dangerous
thieves were those who robbed the mails. They worked in
small groups of two or three and travelled on the trains,
always with an empty suitcase. Whenever they managed to
penetrate the locked mail compartment they took what they
could and crammed it into their empty suitcase, which they
left standing in the corridor well away from their compartment. I regret to say that we never caught the thieves for
those particular jobs, but we knew who they were and were
able to arrest them for other crimes.

Lorry traffic suffered, too, although not to such a great
extent, and that type of theft decreased after my detectives
pounced on a certain fat little man who always wedged the
lorry drivers into a corner of the café where they stopped for
tea so that they were powerless to get out when they saw
their lorry being driven away. He " grassed " (informed)
on the gang, and another nine men went to gaol.

In January, 1945, I was promoted to Detective Superintendent, and took charge of the C.I.D. work in the South

London district for a few months until September of the same year when a vacancy occurred in the North London district, where I lived. This was much more convenient and indeed very considerate of the Authorities. Incidentally, my place in the South Side was taken by my old colleague, Mr. Greeno.

My district comprised five divisions, with over two hundred detectives, and getting on for the same number of young men who were employed in plain clothes with the C.I.D. Officers, and were known as " Aids."

The district was very large and extended from Oxford Street in the West End to Potters Bar in the north, and approximately 15 miles east and west. Quite an area.

CHAPTER NINE

MURDER TRAILS

MY NEW APPOINTMENT was a completely different job from running the Flying Squad, the shock troops of the C.I.D. Here I controlled and supervised the C.I.D. work in all the divisions in my district. It meant visiting the stations frequently, seeing that the books were kept properly up to date, advising in difficult cases and taking charge of some. And for many hours I was chained to my desk reading through reports.

Little is known of the immense amount of paper work which goes hand in hand with detection. There must be a full report on every single job, plus various returns which are used at the Criminal Record Office. I realised just what an onerous task this was for detectives who typed with only two fingers, and then inaccurately, and I, with others, pressed for women typists who later were engaged and so helped speed the necessary returns.

I spent ten years in that district and probed many important crimes, particularly murders. Many of those investigations were successful but some still remain unsolved. One of these was, in a way, more interesting than most and finished up in a blaze of publicity with the crime reporters bending over backwards to find new superlatives with which to eulogise the C.I.D. It began in the fairly uneventful year of 1947. John Edward Allen, the man known as the " Mad Parson," had escaped from Broadmoor, where he was detained after being found guilty of murder. Then a man called Albert Welch disappeared from his home at Potters Bar. Both these events were soon forgotten in a wave of robbery with violence which hit London, and detectives everywhere were working all out to crush this new and savage banditry. Six months went busily by, and then two small boys, walking across the golf course at Potters Bar, saw a hand sticking out of the murky water of a pond.

Those two boys, who had been looking for golf balls, ran hotfoot to the club house and reported what they had seen. They were out of breath and nervous. The steward seemed inclined not to believe them, but he passed on the information to some of the club members, who went to the pond. They saw an arm sticking out of the water and immediately telephoned the police at Potters Bar.

At that stage the finding of an arm did not necessarily point to murder. I remember, years ago, finding a body in a house which turned out to be a preserved cadaver used for instructing students. I thought then that I was on the threshold of my first murder case and was soundly admonished for my ignorance!

Detective Inspector George Brown went from Barnet police station and pulled out the arm. He found that the fingers were beautifully slender and white—they could have belonged to a woman. I drove out at once to the golf course, at the very edge of my territory. I realised that this pond might well yield further secrets and contacted the Thames Police. Within a few hours, I had three men there with a boat and special drags and nets. In two days they found more human remains, this time legs and feet. Each limb had been cut into three portions and it was obvious that there had been nothing accidental about this death. Here was evidence that pointed to brutal murder, dismemberment and disposal.

Detective Chief Inspector MacDougall was in charge of C.I.D. work in this particular division and took over the inquiries. Day by day more human remains were found and the public was fascinated as each grim discovery was reported fully in the newspapers. There must have been at least thirty reporters standing around waiting for the next find. I remember that one evening paper had a radio car designed so that the reporter could send his story direct from the golf course. The skull of the victim was dragged out and all the other reporters ran for telephones. The reporter with the radio car was in no hurry. He stood around and waited for a while, then sauntered across to his car. He picked up his microphone and heard so many atmospherics that he couldn't put his story through, and eventually had to charge after his colleagues. He missed an edition.

All the gruesome remains taken from the pond were handed over to Dr. Donald Teare, the pathologist who so frequently works for Scotland Yard. After some examination he was able to report that the remains were certainly those of a man and that the body had been crudely dismembered, possibly with a hack-saw. He was able to give a fair idea of what the man looked like in life. The interesting point was the hands—whoever the man was, he had kept his nails in first-class condition. That was why the early report suggested that the hand sticking out of the pond was that of a woman.

Dr. Teare was also able to say that the remains of this body had been in the pond for about seven months, probably since the previous November. It was clear that whoever had disposed of this body must have known the district well. To reach the pond from any direction meant a cross-country walk of some distance, and since there was a public footpath across the golf course there would always be a chance of meeting someone unless local knowledge indicated the best time and route.

When all the parts were assembled the body proved to be that of a man of about five feet six inches in height and aged thirty-five to forty-five. There was a hole in the front of his skull, and inside were two small bones suggesting that death was due to a violent blow on the forehead. An immediate check was made of all male persons missing from October in the previous year. There were hundreds, but all were accounted for except Albert Welch, aged forty-five, who had disappeared from his home in Potters Bar on November 17, 1947. Local inquiries suggested that the remains found in the pond might well be those of Welch, but there was no proof.

He was a railway linesman and, strangely, very careful about his hands. On November 17 he had left home but never arrived at work, although he was due, that day, to collect a week's wages.

Fingerprint impressions were taken from the body and a minute search for comparison prints made in his house and in the various places he had worked on the railway. Not a single print could be found and it was left to the Yard laboratory to satisfy the coroner's jury of the identity of the remains found in the pond.

A photograph of Welch was obtained and copies of it and of the skull were superimposed upon one another. The outline and main features showed such a close resemblance that the skull could have been that of Welch. There was also a clue in the teeth, although no teeth were present in the skull. It was checked that Welch's teeth had been extracted long before, but there was an indication of an abscess on the upper jaw. He had complained of pain in his upper jaw just prior to his disappearance. Then a comparison was made between a pair of Welch's boots and the feet found in the pond, and they proved to be accurate beyond the point of doubt.

The coroner's jury found a verdict of wilful murder by a person or persons unknown and named the date as November 17 or 18. They were satisfied that the remains were those of Albert Welch.

There were other cases, too, in which we were unable to make an arrest. In one of them the victim was a woman, who was murdered in Regent's Park, that elegant green oasis so near the luxury of Marylebone and the worst slums of Camden Town.

Miss Gladys Margaret Irene Hanrahan, a book-keeper, aged thirty-five, lived in St. Ervan's Road, North Kensington. She was found on Cumberland Green in Regent's Park, near the Outer Circle, just after ten o'clock one night in October. She had been strangled and a man's handkerchief with a large letter A embroidered on the corner had been forced into her mouth. She was lying perfectly naturally, almost as though she had gone to sleep, and there was no sign of a struggle, and not one of the many people who were going through the park at the time had heard any screams. There was no question of robbery being the motive, for the victim's handbag containing £5 was lying underneath the body, and she was also wearing a valuable ring. Although she had not been criminally assaulted, there were several bruises on her body and one of her fingernails was broken.

The one solid clue was the handkerchief, and immediately a special inquiry was made at all laundries. It was not long before we found the owner of the handkerchief, a neighbour of the victim, but he was able to satisfy us that it had been lost or stolen some time before. He insisted that he was in a seaside town sixty miles away from London on the evening Miss Hanrahan was killed. Despite a close search of the area, Detective Chief Inspector Jamieson and his men could find no other clues to give us a lead.

Miss Hanrahan was a very quiet type of girl, with few men friends, and none of them enjoyed a particularly close relationship. Each evening she left her work and spent several hours helping her uncle who ran an off-licence not very far from her home. We discovered that she sometimes walked through Regent's Park to visit friends in the district,

but it was established that she did not call on any of them
on the night she was found dead. It was clear, from what
we could find out from witnesses, that she had left home on
the day of the murder saying she was going to the cinema.

It was possible, I reasoned, that she had been killed by
some man with whom she had a secret appointment, or
perhaps that she had been followed. On the other hand, a
man who attacks a strange woman usually has a sexual
motive which leaves its mark. I engaged every single
detective available in the hope of solving this crime,
and Superintendent Birch, then deputy head of the Yard's
Fingerprint Department, tried for days to get some kind of
fingerprint from a slight impression of the skin of the dead
woman's throat. We tried this because in previous cases
we had sometimes managed to achieve some kind of success.

A little later, a man and his wife got into touch with us
and said that they thought they had seen Miss Hanrahan
in a large saloon car in Regent's Park, and that they had seen
her on successive nights; we could obtain no corrobora-
tion, but it was quite clear to my mind that she had been
killed by someone she knew. We interviewed every single
man of her acquaintance, but they were all able to give a
perfectly satisfactory explanation as to what they were
doing on that particular day. Always in a crime like this
there are many hidden things which never come to the
surface, and indeed this was another occasion where we did
discover some of the things which might have helped us,
but could obtain no proof.

It is disturbing to a police officer to have an unsolved
murder on his hands, but it must happen sometimes. It is
even more disturbing to be ninety-nine per cent. certain of
knowing the identity of the killer and still unable to arrest
him. I have been in that position several times, and the
suspect has known it.

Every murder is a new and different puzzle, and successful
investigation means hours of experience, skill and patience.
Very few killers get away with it, for the bodies of their
victims have an embarrassing habit of turning up, and a
dead body can tell a number of tales.

The murderers who most frequently escape detection are
perhaps the most frightening, those guilty of sex crimes.
The reason is plain. They are not premeditated but committed entirely on the spur of the moment, and unless the
murderer is caught in the act or leaves something behind
there is very little chance of detection. You may recall
some of the many unsolved sex murders of recent years,
quite often children, where the killers were never seen
either before or afterwards. These authors of sex crimes
have always seemed to have the most phenomenal luck in
never leaving anything incriminating behind them, and
seemingly able to escape without anyone ever seeing anything of them or even suspecting them. Any police officer
will tell you that the chances of catching even the most
juvenile sex offender are very slim although there have been
many arrests for such crimes throughout the country.

Fortunately, such crimes are relatively rare. Few murderers, until they are faced with the terrible moment of
arrest, have any real appreciation of the complicated and
delicately meshed machinery that has been brought to bear
against them from the moment their crime was discovered.
And the general public—through sensational films and
lurid works of fiction—also forms a somewhat distorted
picture of the methods and mental equipment of investigating officers. The average detective is neither a superman
nor a clumsy policeman who works haphazardly in the
dark, relying on good luck or the chance tip from an
informer.

I have mentioned the Murder Bag, which is rather
like a suitcase of heavy leather, containing every article

which an investigator might need in probing a killing. It contains the following: fingerprint oufit; metal foot-print forma; twenty-four inch boxwood rule, sixty-six foot measuring tape; two metric rules; map measure; compass; torch; pencil torch with reflector; lenses; clinical thermometer; scissors; probes; lancets; pliers; tweezers; test tubes; glass boxes; standard thermometer; small cardboard boxes; overalls; rubber apron; rubber gloves; disinfectants; soap-box; sponge; towels; napkins; brief-case; statement paper; adhesive and transparent tape; envelopes; pocket-books; labels; and handcuffs.

Probing murder is an exact science and no chances can be taken, for the slightest error is pounced upon by the defence and a great deal made of it. It is necessary therefore to label all exhibits when they are found, and to record the name of the officer who found them, and their exact location. The detective must remember that, at the end of his investigation, which may take many months, he has to prepare a report which will contain all that is known of the crime, and one that must stand up to minute examination years afterwards.

It is always a good rule when faced with a case of sudden death to suspect the worst, that is, murder. There are times when the circumstances give an overwhelming impression of suicide or accident, but those cases must be investigated with perhaps an even more jaundiced eye than something that looks straightforward. Remember that a murderer may have had plenty of time and ample opportunity to arrange things in order to deceive the investigator. It is vital, therefore, quickly to answer the following questions: What is the cause of death? Could the person have inflicted the injuries himself? Are there any signs of a struggle? Where is the weapon or object which caused the injuries?

If at the scene of the crime there are distinct signs of a

struggle, then it can be assumed from the start that another person was involved. In a room the signs of a struggle usually consist of blood-stains, hair, overturned furniture, rumpled carpets, and marks of weapons and injuries caused by the dead person defending himself. It is possible to tell from the marks of a struggle whether the attacked person retreated, or whichever way he moved. Blood marks give help in reconstructing what happened. The victim does not necessarily become immediately unconscious, and as he moves around the room, trying to ward off the attack, he touches various articles and leaves blood marks upon them. The pattern of blood upon a wall, too, gives an indication of which way the blow was struck.

When examining on the scene of a crime, I always looked carefully for blood marks on doors, telephones, clothes and curtains. Spattered blood can show how far a drawer or piece of furniture was pulled out, or whether the doors of a cupboard were open during the struggle. There may be a footprint in blood. Usually such a mark is blurred, but it may be possible to decide whether it was made by the victim or the attacker.

The position of the furniture also gives a fair indication of the direction of the struggle, and sometimes of the route by which the victim attempted to escape, or the route used by the criminal to get away. Furniture falls in the direction of the movement. There are times, of course, when a criminal has righted overturned furniture and thus left a fingerprint clue.

In cases of death by violence out of doors, marks of a struggle are less distinct, but there may be broken-off twigs or trodden-down leaves, and footmarks at a place little used by walkers. There may also be blood-stains on grass or bushes and hair adhering to bushes or twigs.

Clues are found in all sorts of places. There may be something to be learned from the position of the curtains, or the date on papers in the letter-box, and if they are in the right order of delivery. There may be clothing and other objects which do not belong to the residents in the house, or the lamps may be alight when the crime is discovered. Something can be told from the reading of the electricity or gas meters, such as how long it is since they were used, and therefore how long the person in the house has been dead.

Fireplaces are important. There may be ash or burnt residues which will yield some helpful clue. I always remember the late Sir Bernard Spilsbury arriving at the scene of a murder, and he taught me one important thing among many others. As soon as he arrived in the room he would ask everyone to be still, and then he would stand and sniff for several minutes, to see if he could detect any odour. He could have smelt possibly gas or gunpowder, tobacco fumes or alcohol, or even perfume, but such odours soon disappear and, if not detected immediately, are lost for ever.

It is vital, too, to look at clocks and watches, and in particular alarm clocks. There may be signs of a celebration, bottles of alcohol, glasses of different kinds which may carry fingerprints. Cigarette ends and matches may help, and also the remains of smoked tobacco.

Criminals, even when committing crimes they have carefully prepared, make all sorts of small mistakes. I can remember cases where criminals have discarded a newspaper with their own address on it, or thrown away a piece of paper which gives some clue to their identity. They may have used the water closet, or washed their hands in the kitchen or bathroom and left a mark there. Criminals have ingrained habits, such as taking off a ring before they wash; the ring may have been left behind. It is usually possible to tell whether a victim undressed himself or was undressed by the murderer. This more frequently happens in the case of women, but it is possible to find out the order in

which a person takes off his or her garments, and possibly
to tell by the way they are found whether they were taken
off in that order or a different one. Here again the habits
of the victim may prove the undoing of the criminal.

Practically every trade has what we detectives call an
" occupational " mark. By these means it is possible to tell
with a fair degree of accuracy the job of either the victim of
a crime or the criminal. For instance, a tailor has the marks
and scars of needle punctures in the tip of the left index
finger. A shoemaker has round hollows in the front teeth
from biting the thread, and they also have the marks on their
left thumb-nails. Photographers, and sometimes chemists,
have brittle nails which are often discoloured. Bricklayers
have a hardening of their right hand from gripping the
trowel, and the skin of the left hand is worn thin from
holding the bricks. Painters, too, have callouses on their
fingers from gripping the handle of the brush, and coal-
workers have small particles of coal embedded in the skin.

Watches often give a clue to identity because they sometimes have marks on them from their last repair. In the same
way an examination of the teeth can be most valuable.
Most dentists keep charts of all their patients. It happened,
I well remember, in the Christie case, in which I was involved for the first three days while Chief Superintendent
Tom Barratt was on leave. There we had found various
remains in the house in Rillington Place, Notting Hill, and
it was possible to identify one of the victims by certain
fillings in the teeth. Even teeth missing from the jaw can
help in narrowing down the search for identity.

All these clues finish up at the Yard, where the experts,
the back-room boys, can assess their value. Among them
are the fingerprint detectives. Every time a man or woman
is arrested in this country for a crime, and has no objections,
a set of his or her fingerprints is taken on a special form and
sent up to the Criminal Record Office. They are recorded

by detectives, who roll the fingers on an inked copper plate and then roll the impression from the finger on to white paper. Those forms arrive by every post at the Yard and urgent ones are taken by hand. An immediate check through records is made and, if the accused person is known, the dossier goes out to the detective concerned.

This is a phenomenal task and involves the most accurate work. Indeed, so accurate is the business of fingerprints that no detective officer employed there is allowed to give expert fingerprint evidence in court unless he has served seven years in the Fingerprint Department.

As the technique for taking fingerprints developed, so has the technique for finding them at the scene of the crime. Once a print is found, it is photographed and then compared with those in the records. Prints have been found on practically every kind of surface, and indeed the science does not stop merely at fingerprints, for people have been hanged after leaving part of a palm print at the scene of a crime. One rogue tried very hard to make sure that the police would never catch him through his fingerprints—he picked off the flesh of all his fingers and so destroyed the patterns of his fingerprints. This worked for a while, but eventually the skin grew again and back came the original pattern—his suffering, which lasted for some eighteen months, was completely in vain.

Before leaving the subject of fingerprints, I must point out that any fingerprint taken of a person who is subsequently found not guilty is destroyed. There was a recent case, possibly well within your memory and soon after I had left the Yard, where thousands of people volunteered to have their fingerprints taken. Eventually a youth was arrested and found guilty of the particular crime, and those thousands of fingerprint forms were publicly destroyed.

Working very closely with the Fingerprint Department is the Photographic Section, which is in the charge of one of the most astute men in the Metropolitan Police. His name is Superintendent Percy Law, a long, lean character who has perfected many inventions. At every major crime you will find him or one of his men taking the necessary pictures to record the scene exactly. And there are very few major murders in the last twenty years which Superintendent Law has not attended and recorded in clean-cut photographs, and very few courts in which his photographs have not been used to show the jury just how the police found things when they arrived.

Remember that many marks found at the scene of a crime are fugitive, but the camera records them. Many a cruel murder has been solved in the room Superintendent Law occupies high above the Thames.

All kinds of forgeries find their way into the Photographic Department. There have been criminals who have forged postage stamps, insurance stamps, clothing coupons—particularly during the war—and many such cases were detected by Superintendent Law and his men. Forged cheques which frequently come to light, having been stolen from delivery boxes, quickly forged and presented at the bank, are detected by the camera with the use of the microscope and the ultra-violet rays. Writing, sometimes obliterated by paint or some other thick substance, can be detected by infra-red rays, and many a thief who thought he was safe has been caught by these means. Even charred remains of paper, found at the scene of a crime, which years ago would have been disregarded as useless have been carefully collected and photographs taken to show up the original writing on the paper.

Not far from where Superintendent Law gets through so much important work is the Forensic Laboratory, one of the most up-to-date in the world. Its use has become enormous over recent years, particularly in cases of serious crime, and especially in murder. In every case of murder the clothes of the victim, and possibly the rugs, curtains and some of the furniture, are sent to the Forensic Laboratory to see what can be found. Very often a vacuum cleaner is used at the scene of a crime and the contents of the bag afterwards analysed by the chemists. It is amazing what they find. Clothes pick up all kinds of dust and other particles which cannot be seen by the naked eye but are easily apparent under the microscope. The turn-ups of a man's trousers collect an extraordinary assortment of specimens of dust and fluff which can enable a scientist to tell accurately where he has been, and in some cases what he has been doing. In the laboratory they have a checking system on all kinds of dust, fibres, woods and metals, which enables them to identify the source of any particular type of dust in a very short time indeed.

There must be hundreds of cases on record, and I know of many myself in which I was concerned, when the chemists have found blood-stains which we detectives could not see. Criminals have been known to wash their clothes, not once but many times, in strong solutions of soap and ammonia, but even then the chemists still manage to find blood traces. The examinations they make are in great detail. They take a pair of shoes to pieces and examine every single part; clothes are taken apart by the seams and thoroughly examined and tested. The various tell-tale traces on a man's clothing, like the inside of the hatband, the inside of the cuffs, the shirt cuffs, the front of the jacket, the flaps of the pockets and inside the pockets—such clues have led to the downfall of many a vicious killer.

Criminals today have a very real fear of the Forensic Laboratory. Burglars have felt hungry while working in the house of their victim and decided to take a bite at an apple or a piece of cheese and have then forgotten the apple or the cheese and left it behind. The scientists make a plaster impression of that bite, and later when the suspect is arrested he may be given an apple to eat. The bite is compared with that found at the scene of the crime.

You may have read in evidence many times that skin under a victim's fingernails has helped to convict a man. As so often happens in cases of violence, the victim struggles and scratches his attacker, usually on the face. Under the nails will be particles of skin, and also blood which can be grouped. Hairs have been found on a suspect which the Yard scientists have been able to measure up with those of the victim, although the crime may have been committed many weeks or even months before. They do the same thing with woollen or cotton fibres, or fibres from a rug or a carpet.

This department also tackles cases of poisoning. Every time there is an exhumation, Superintendent George Salter, who is the Yard liaison officer with the scientists, attends and takes from the pathologist the necessary specimens which are to be analysed. There again, in the laboratory, they have every known poison which can be compared with any poison found in the body.

The science of toxicology is developing all the time. With the remarkable advance in the discovery of new drugs, police scientists have to keep up to date and remain alert for ingenious devices by poisoners who rarely commit their crimes without a coldly premeditated plan of action.

CHAPTER TEN

DEATH ON THE BEAT

IN JANUARY, 1948, housebreaking was very prevalent around the Southgate area and much valuable property was being stolen. After discussion it was agreed between District Headquarters, Mr. Frith, the Divisional Superintendent, and the Divisional Detective Inspector, Mr. Stinton, that a team of uniformed constables would be selected to patrol the neighbourhood in plain clothes during the evenings. This was accordingly put into effect.

The men patrolled in pairs and were given certain streets. If they decided to split up, one could walk on either side of the street, but at all times they had orders to be within reasonable distance of one another in case either of them needed assistance, and to secure corroborative evidence. Occasionally, of course, the pair did lose sight of one another for a short period, particularly when doubling round a couple of streets, and they would meet at the other end. Above all, their orders were to be as inconspicuous as possible, and in long wide streets of imposing houses this was difficult.

At ten o'clock on the night of February 13, 1948, I was alerted by telephone, this time by Divisional Detective Inspector Stinton. He told me the bad news that one of the men selected for this anti-burglar night patrol had been shot dead. He was P.C. Nathaniel Edgar.

Understandably such a case is always the more personal kind of investigation when a police officer has been murdered. I was told that at about eight o'clock that evening P.C. Edgar and his colleague had parted in the hope of locating a suspect whom they had earlier seen lurking around Southgate tube station. Not long after that a Mrs. Laing dialled 999 and reported that, while she was out walking with her brother, she had heard three shots, and almost at once seen a man run along Broadfields Avenue from Wade's Hill and disappear. She and her brother ran into Wade's Hill and in a garage entrance of No. 112 saw P.C. Edgar lying on the ground. He was groaning and bleeding profusely. They did what they could to comfort him, and, meanwhile, a wireless car had picked up the message from the Information Room and was going fast towards Wade's Hill.

The crew jumped out and one of them held Edgar up by the shoulders while the others tore his clothes off and tried to staunch the bleeding from his wounds. Edgar was by this time slipping fast into unconsciousness, but managed to murmur into the ear of one of the car crew: " The man was by the door. I got his identity card and name. He shot me in the legs with three shots. The pocket-book is in my inside pocket." To say these words meant a tremendous effort of will-power, and it was in the true tradition of the policeman that he managed to pass on the information before he finally became insensible. He never came to again, and died soon after reaching hospital despite the local doctor's strenuous efforts.

When the officers took his pocket-book they saw the following entry: " M (or Mr.) Thomas, Donald, 247 Cambridge Road, Enfield, BEAH 257/2." They drove straight to the police station and handed this pocket-book in to Mr. Stinton. In hospital the doctors found that Edgar had been shot three times and had wounds in the right groin and thigh.

Stinton at once sent for the man who had been working with Edgar, but, unfortunately, he had been round another corner at the time and so had not seen what had happened.

He was able to say that they had spotted a man acting suspiciously, and he gave a certain description of him. Meanwhile, Stinton got on to the Criminal Record Office and gave them the particulars which he had found in Edgar's notebook. It took them but a few seconds to identify the " Thomas " in Edgar's notebook as Donald George Thomas, a deserter wanted since October 13, 1947. They gave an address in Enfield.

Usually the police have no particular feeling against criminals, and over the years they develop a considerable understanding of how criminals think, and how they react to the normal strain of life. They also consider the early environment of some of these criminals, and make certain allowances for their behaviour. This time every man in the station, and indeed the whole of the Metropolitan Police, would have worked every minute of every day for as long as it took to find the man responsible for that murder.

Edgar was thirty-three and had joined the Metropolitan Police in 1939. Later he had volunteered for service in the Royal Navy, and had returned to police duties in 1946. He was married and had two small boys. He came from Fife, and I knew that his younger brother had been captured with the 51st Highland Division at St. Valéry, and later, with a young French girl, had made a daring escape right through France and into Spain. Mrs. Edgar, who had expected her husband home later that night, was told of the tragedy; perhaps the worst duty a police officer is ever called upon to perform.

Detectives went round to Thomas's address in Cambridge Road, Enfield, but, as they expected, he was not there. Inquiries went on throughout the night, and it was learned that Thomas had become infatuated with the wife of another local man, and that she was missing from home. It was reasonable to suppose that this woman was now living with Thomas somewhere in London. I saw the husband of this woman and, early on the following morning, obtained a photograph of his wife. I kept this quiet until the late afternoon, because it was my intention that this photograph should be published in the newspapers. I was absolutely certain that Thomas and this woman were somewhere in London, possibly living in a furnished room, and I wanted that photograph to be in the morning and not the evening papers. During the later afternoon I took the photograph to Scotland Yard and saw my immediate superior. At first he did not agree with my idea, but discussed it with the Commissioner, Sir Harold Scott, and Sir Ronald Howe. This was breaking fresh ground in a case of murder, and it was a point that had to be considered very carefully; but, after considerable and friendly argument, it was agreed that the photograph should be published in the morning papers in the hope that someone would recognise it. The Press Bureau at the Yard was instructed accordingly, and the result was that all the morning papers published the woman's photograph, together with a paragraph to the effect that she might be found in the company of the man, Thomas.

For the first time, we issued to the Press the form of words which has since become familiar, stating that the police urgently wished to interview Donald George Thomas who, it was believed, could help them in their inquiries into the murder of P.C. Edgar.

Reproductions of the woman's photograph appeared in the morning editions of February 17, and at half past seven that morning a Mrs. Smeed, who kept a boarding house in Clapham, saw the photograph and showed it to her husband, saying she thought it was that of a woman who was then sharing their top front room with a man. Mr. Smeed looked at the photograph and went straight to find a police officer and told him of their suspicions. The officer, as keen as the other serving London policemen on helping to find

Thomas, immediately told the Information Room, and meantime kept watch on the house. In less than three minutes a wireless car arrived with three officers, followed shortly afterwards by Inspector Moodie from Brixton police station.

Moodie, who played goalkeeper for the Metropolitan Police first eleven for many years, was an extremely powerful man. He took charge of the situation, and with the other officers from the wireless car, which was parked some distance away so as not to be noticed, crept into the house and saw Mrs. Smeed in the kitchen. She remembered that she had been asked to take tea to the couple in their room that morning, and the inspector told her to carry on just as though nothing had happened. As she walked up with the tea-tray he followed, and the other officers were close behind. Mrs. Smeed laid the tray on the floor, knocked at the door, and heard a man's voice inside say " O.K.," and then she went downstairs. The officers waited, tense, outside the door until they heard the key turn in the lock. The door opened minutely, and Thomas, dressed in his vest and pants, looked through the crack. He saw the officers and slammed the door, but they charged against it and got in. As they did so, Thomas made a leap for the bed and put his hand under the pillow.

Moodie, who was in the lead, flung his sixteen stone on Thomas and seized his right hand, which held a gun. The other officers grabbed Thomas, and there was a short violent struggle until the gun was wrenched from his hand and he was under control.

The inspector cautioned Thomas and asked: " Is the gun loaded ? "

" That gun's full up," Thomas replied, " and they were all for you."

The officers took him downstairs to the car which had been brought up outside the door, and on the way to the station he said: " You were lucky. I might just as well be hung for a sheep as a lamb."

A message was sent out to me, and Stinton and his officers went across to the boarding house to search the room. There they found seventeen rounds of ·35 ammunition, a rubber truncheon, a jemmy, a number of identity cards and an instruction book called *Shooting to Live with a One-Hand Gun*. Published in 1942 it was written by two ex-Commandos, Captains Fairburn and Sykes, and described, according to the preface, " methods developed and practised during an uneventful quarter of a century and adopted in spite of their unorthodoxy by one police organisation after another in the Far East and elsewhere. It is the authors' hope that the relation of these methods may contribute to the efficiency and therefore safety of those whose lot it is to use the one-hand gun in the course of duty." There were chapter headings in the book: " Purposes of the Pistol "; " Choosing a Pistol "; " Training— Preliminary Course for Recruits "; and " Training— Advanced Methods."

The automatic wrenched from Thomas's hand was a Luger, and when examined at the police station it contained eight rounds in the magazine and one in the breech. The woman, who had been in bed in the room when Thomas was arrested, told my officers that Thomas had confessed to her that he had shot Edgar. He was taken from Brixton across to Southgate, where I saw him. He was a dark, tough-looking young man and extremely truculent. He refused to say anything about the night of February 13, except to give a false account of his movements.

The gun was sent to the Yard laboratory, and tests made there proved clearly that the bullets found in Edgar's body had been fired from it.

As in the case of all prisoners, we had to investigate Thomas's background. We discovered that he was born in July, 1925, and had been to school in Edmonton, where he was classed intellectually among the top boys. He left when he was fourteen, after being captain of the cricket eleven and a member of the local Boys' Brigade. He started work as a telegraph messenger and then became a junior clerk, and was first in trouble with the police just before his sixteenth birthday. He was given twelve months' probation, but then committed further offences, mostly of theft, and was sent to an approved school. When he left there he began to study mathematics and electrical engineering at a technical school, and was called up for military service in January, 1945, only a few months before the war ended. But he deserted in two weeks, and after two years on the run surrendered to the military police and served 160 days' detention. Very soon after his release he deserted again and had been absent just over three months when he shot P.C. Edgar.

At his trial Thomas was found guilty of murder and ordered to be detained during His Majesty's pleasure.

From Thomas in the witness-box the full story finally came out. He described how, on the evening of February 13, he went to Southgate to look at some property. He was stopped by P.C. Edgar, who asked him for his name and identity number.

These he gave to the officer, who then searched him, but he did not find the gun which Thomas always carried strapped in front of him in his belt. P.C. Edgar was not satisfied with Thomas's answers, who said he would take the officer to friends he had visited at Wade's Hill. In fact he had no friends there and this was merely a bluff to gain time.

Together they went by bus to Winchmore Hill and to the house at Wade's Hill. When they got outside Thomas knew his bluff had been called and thought about escaping. He knew he was wanted by the Army as a deserter and was afraid of getting three years' imprisonment if he was discovered. He looked round for a way of escape, but there was none, so he pulled his gun from his belt and pointed it at P.C. Edgar, who closed with him and caught hold of the barrel. The constable pushed the gun to point towards the ground and it went off. Then P.C. Edgar bent on one knee, still holding the barrel, and a second bullet entered his body. He then fell forward and, with his hand holding the gun twisted behind his back, a third shot was fired.

Thomas was handed a brown leather strap by a warder and, strapping this about his waist, demonstrated how he always carried the gun stuck in the front of it with his coat buttoned up over it.

" I had no intention of killing P.C. Edgar," he asserted. " I pulled the gun to scare him."

He was typical of the young gangster who invaded the streets of London in the years following the war. The reason he carried a gun, fully loaded, was, according to himself, to impress his friends. It impressed them more if it was loaded, he said; apparently guns fascinated him, and he had worked as a toolmaker and studied the mechanism of weapons. He found it easier to impress his personality on his friends if he could pull a loaded gun from his belt.

Thomas, at the time of his arrest, had seven different identity cards. It might well have been that, had he produced a different one to that in his own name, he might have been more difficult to catch. When he left school he resented having to work, and one day when his mother found a pound missing she called in the police. They were more interested in two bicycles they found there. So, before he was sixteen, Thomas had begun the slippery slide into a criminal career. He stole another bicycle, and then did his spell in an approved school. His spare time was spent in pin-table saloons and back-street cafés talking to other young toughs.

This murder had a profound effect upon the public conscience. Long before Thomas came to trial funds had been set up for Edgar's widow and children. The *News of the World* announced this fund, and it was followed by various organisations all over the country.

One last word on this case. It was a perfect example of co-operation between the police, the Press and the public. In the first place it was a member of the public, Mrs. Laing, who heard the shooting and telephoned the Information Room, which brought a wireless car there within a few minutes. The police were by no means slow in their inquiries, and, finally, having obtained a picture of the woman with whom Thomas was living, the Press co-operated to the full and used it exactly at the requested time, which resulted in an early arrest without further loss of life.

*   *   *

While the Potters Bar murder was still being investigated, at the beginning of June, 1948, I was sent for by the Assistant Commissioner for Crime, Sir Ronald Howe, who told me that he had received a request from the Home Office for the services of two experienced detective officers to go to South America to assist in an investigation at Bogotá, Colombia. Sir Ronald explained that there had been a revolution in Bogotá some weeks earlier and this would be the subject of the inquiry, but merely in an advisory capacity. He asked me if I was prepared to go, and, if so, to select another officer to accompany me.

He assured me that it was a most unusual thing for a British police officer to be asked to go to a foreign country, and considered it a high compliment both to Britain and to the Metropolitan Police. I assured him that I realised my responsibility and would take my old colleague, now Inspector Albert Tansill.

There were discussions with various Home Office and

Foreign Office officials, and I was told that there had been a revolution on April 9 of that year in the heart of the city of Bogotá, following the murder of Dr. Jorge Eliecer Gaitan, leader of the extreme left wing of the Liberal Party. Many hundreds of people had lost their lives. At the time of this revolution the Pan-American Conference was being held in Bogotá, and it was rumoured that the murder of Dr. Gaitan was political. He had been associated with the Liberals, and although its parties were excluded from suspicion the Conservatives, and largely the Communists, were under suspicion by certain sections of the public, mostly of Spanish or Indian extraction. My duties were merely to assist their own investigation staff, which was already appointed, and had in fact already commenced work.

I was told that Inspector Tansill and myself would be joined by Sir Norman Smith, C.I.E., O.B.E., ex-Indian Police, and former Director of the Intelligence Bureau of the Government of India.

Inspector Tansill and I flew from London Airport on June 11, called briefly at Prestwick, and flew on to New York, where we were joined by Sir Norman Smith. We met up in New York with some of their policemen, many of them originally from Ireland, and were given a magnificent sightseeing tour. Next morning we left for Miami, but savoured none of the world-famous attractions because a heavy storm broke and we were forced to stay in our hotel.

The next day, after a short call at Cuba, we arrived at Bogotá and were met by the British Ambassador, Sir Gilbert Mackereth, and members of his staff.

We were given an interpreter, a British subject, a beautiful apartment, and a cook and general servant to attend to our wants. We were warned that, since Bogotá was 9,000 feet above sea level, the altitude could be trying, and were urged not to be too energetic when climbing stairs. I only refused the elevator once—fifteen stone is a lot to carry at high altitudes.

Since the revolution, all police duties in the city had been taken over by the military, and there was a curfew in existence, which meant that all unauthorised persons had to be clear of the streets by midnight. It was suggested to us that in the circumstances we might wish to be armed, but this we declined. Sir Norman, on the other hand, was all for it and tried to make us change our minds. However, we stuck to our decision, probably wisely, since neither of us had handled a gun for many years.

We were introduced to Dr. Ricardo Jordan, who had been specially appointed by the Colombian Government to investigate the death of Dr. Gaitan, and from then on worked with him. All the statements, which had been very thoroughly taken, were put at our disposal, and we began to go through them. It was agreed beforehand that all this work was highly confidential, and that no information would be divulged to anyone. Dr. Jordan was a lawyer, a magistrate and a judge, and an extremely intelligent man. We visited his office each day and went right through the case with him.

The statements of the witnesses were quite clear and had all been taken, according to the custom of the country, under oath. Briefly the story was this. Shortly after 1 p.m. on April 9, Dr. Gaitan with three friends descended from his office on the third floor of a large building to the ground floor. They were going to lunch. As they reached street level and walked to the door there was the report of a revolver and then several other shots, and Dr. Gaitan fell, mortally wounded. He had been shot in the back. The witnesses, including Dr. Gaitan's three friends, all spoke of seeing the assassin, of whom they were able to give a full description. The man was arrested almost immediately by two police officers who were nearby, and the revolver taken from him. What happened after that, however, was most unfortunate, but perhaps typical of the population, and undoubtedly the cause of the serious trouble which followed.

According to the witnesses, the police officers were doing their job perfectly efficiently until the crowd suddenly grew restive, got completely out of hand and wrenched the assassin from the grasp of the two policemen. In seconds the street was full of a howling mass of people, and somewhere in the middle was the prisoner. When the crowd was eventually dispersed the prisoner was found on the ground. He had been battered to death. The crowd's mood was so fierce, and their blows so vicious, that the assassin's features were mutilated to the point that recognition was almost impossible. More police were called and the body was removed to the mortuary.

This riot, which resulted in a killing, spread throughout the city, and the police were completely powerless to control it. All that night and the next day enormous crowds rioted, looted buildings, and set fire to motor-cars and houses. The damage was enormous but, even worse, because of this wave of lawlessness many innocent people were trampled to death.

Dr. Jordan, the investigator, had taken an enormous number of statements, but there was nothing in any of them to point a finger at any political party having been directly responsible for the murder of Dr. Gaitan. On the other hand, there was ample evidence to show who the assassin was—a follower of Dr. Gaitan's party. He was identified as Juan Roa Sierra, aged twenty-six and a native of the city. His body had been identified by various members of his family, including his mother, by means of a ring he was wearing, and articles of clothing which, although torn to ribbons, were still identifiable. In particular they recognised a slight deformity in his body.

I was perfectly satisfied that he had been properly identified and was the man responsible. Further inquiries established that Sierra was suffering from megalomania, witnesses also asserted that he told them he believed that he was a far greater man than Gaitan, and the reincarnation of the founder of Bogotá. In addition, it was discovered that a brother of Sierra had been detained for the past eight years in an asylum. There was also evidence to prove without doubt that Sierra had bought the revolver and bullets in Bogotá on the day previous to the shooting.

These were the findings of Dr. Jordan, and we were in full agreement. To give an idea of the volume of statements in this case, it had taken us six weeks to go through them, examine them, and check one against the other. At each weekend we had been entertained by the Ambassador and his lady and other members of his staff and their wives, and we met several well-known Bogotán families. They took us around the country at weekends and showed us the beauties that were so near to hand. It was two months later when we arrived back in London, and I went back to my headquarters at Paddington, back to my three hundred detectives and my enormous area. In a way I was sorry to leave, for it had been a most fascinating trip; but on the other hand the Olympic Games were about to begin at Wembley, and the Stadium was part of my district.

CHAPTER ELEVEN

THE MAN FROM BAGHDAD

MURDER BEGINS IN a variety of ways. Sometimes there is a fight, the flash of knives or the report of a gun; sometimes the sinister pattern of the poisoner or the smouldering of jealousy that erupts into sudden death.

The story of this murder begins quietly with a prosaic entry by a uniformed officer in the Missing Persons Register which stated that one Stanley Setty had not returned home. It turned out to be one of the most brutal and calculated murders of modern times. It also made criminal history.

The report came into the desk at Albany Street police station, near Regent's Park, at 12.45 p.m. on October 5, 1949. One of Setty's relatives said that the missing man was aged forty-six and had not been to his Bayswater home in Maitland Court since leaving for business the previous morning.

Setty was a kerbside car-dealer in Warren Street, a narrow cobble-stoned thoroughfare just behind Tottenham Court Road where cars are often bought and sold for cash. He had been there on October 4, and disappeared some time during the evening, but there was nothing particularly suspicious about that, at first.

As Chief Superintendent of the area, I was not immediately concerned. Local C.I.D. men made some inquiries and it was reported that Setty's car had been found in the mews running between Albany Street and Regent's Park, where he normally garaged, but with the ignition key missing. My detectives found out that, whenever Setty was late, he left the car outside the garage rather than make a noise by lifting the heavy roller shutter on the garage door. When he did that he always left the ignition key in the car.

The missing key was disturbing and so was the position of the car some way from where Setty left it normally. A further inquiry in Warren Street produced a witness who said he had seen Setty driving his car at 5.50 p.m. on October 4, and there was another man, whom he could not describe, sitting beside him. I had just heard the news and was wondering what had happened when the telephone rang. I picked it up and Bert Tansill said: " Guv'nor, you've heard that Setty is missing. I've had a tip that he may have been murdered."

" How do you know, Bert? " I asked.

"A 'snout' has told me Setty was carrying a lot of cash."

" O.K. Keep in touch and let me know anything you hear." I rang off.

Having a high regard for Tansill's abilities, I ordered some of my detectives to start a quiet probe, and noticed that the crime reporters, with their instinct for a good story, were also on the scent. Very soon I discovered that Setty had told some other person in Warren Street that he intended to visit Watford by car on the night he vanished and had £1,000 in five-pound notes in his pocket. The presence of such a large sum of money made me suspicious and inclined to think that Tansill's information was possibly correct and that Setty had been the victim of foul play.

A telegram was sent to all stations giving a full description of Setty and the fact that he was last seen in his Citroen car at 5.50 p.m. on the 4th, and that the car had since been found abandoned at 1.45 a.m. on the following day near Setty's garage in Chester Place, Regent's Park. He was wearing a blue pin-striped suit, no hat and a cream silk shirt. The same message went to Interpol for circulation all over the world.

I also discovered that the car he proposed to buy was a

3½-litre Jaguar, the property of a person who had recently died.

The newspapers soon got hold of the story and the relatives of Setty offered a reward of £1,000 for recovery of the body, dead or alive. Each day the stories grew bigger, and almost every paper carried a picture of the missing man, but still there was no news of him.

From all over the country reports began to come in that Stanley Setty had been seen. Every one was followed up, but without useful result. Setty had vanished and there was little more we could do about it at that time.

It was known that he had served a term of imprisonment for obtaining credit whilst still an undischarged bankrupt, and we also knew that he was born in Baghdad in 1903 and christened Sulman. He had made his money by trading, but when he had gone bankrupt his debts amounted to nearly £15,000. After his prison sentence he came to London, from Manchester, and started in the business of buying and selling motor-cars. It was well known that he made a lot of money and it was rumoured that he sometimes acted as a moneylender—at a hefty profit.

My inquiries and those of the detectives working under me took us all over London as far as Southend, to Manchester, to Blackpool, to the East End and to Brighton, to the racecourses and the many dog tracks of London. I found that hundreds of people knew Stanley Setty—" Honest Stan " they called him—but none of them wanted to say much about him, and certainly none of them vouchsafed any information which was of the slightest use to me. Chief Inspector Jamieson, who was immediately in charge of the inquiry, found out the numbers of the missing notes, which were circulated.

I had to wait until much later in October to turn the case of a missing man into one of murder. It was on the night of Friday, October 22, just eighteen days after Setty disappeared, that his body was washed up on the mud-flats at Tillingham Marshes, Essex. Sidney Tiffin, a forty-seven-year-old wildfowler, who was out fishing, saw a suspicious bundle and dragged it into his boat and then rowed to shore and told the police. It was, in fact, a dis-membered torso without a head. The torso was wrapped in felt rather like that used under carpets and it had been sewn round the corpse and tied with string.

The first task was to make quite sure that this torso was indeed that of Stanley Setty. Accordingly, fingerprints were taken from the dead man's hands and rushed to Scotland Yard. Once again the efficiency of the Criminal Record Office was demonstrated. A very quick check told them that the prints were identical with those in the file of the man who had once served a term of imprisonment, Stanley Setty. The murder hunt was on.

Dr. Camps, that quiet pipe-smoking pathologist, was called in. He reported that Setty's arms had been tied behind his back and the legs severed by cutting through the trousers and underpants. On the torso was a shirt and an undervest with braces attached to the trousers. Dr. Camps decided that Setty had not been dead more than forty-hours before being placed in the water. There were six distinct stab wounds in the chest which had, of course, penetrated through the shirt and vest. The ribs were fractured. The pathologist estimated that the body had been in the water approximately twenty-one days.

Everything pointed to the fact that the murder could have been committed on the night of October 4, the night Setty had disappeared. We knew that his car, in which he had been seen that evening, had not travelled far before being abandoned in London. It was, therefore, reasonable to suppose that the murder had been committed in London. We had to find out where, and by whose hand.

An interesting point now arose. Here we had a London

inquiry into a missing person, with foul play suspected, but the body, or part of it, had been found in Essex. Scotland Yard officers cannot work in the counties without permission. Detective Superintendent Totterdale of the Essex Constabulary came to London on the night the body was found and it was agreed that Essex would formally ask the Yard for assistance. Accordingly, Superintendent Colin MacDougall (now Chief Superintendent) and Sergeant Neil Sutherland (now Chief Inspector) of the Murder Squad were sent to Essex to take charge there while Chief Inspector John Jamieson carried on with me in London.

Dr. Camps quickly conducted a post-mortem and found out that injuries to the body could only have been caused in one way. It must have been dropped from an aeroplane. He knew this, because, during the war, he had examined the bodies of airmen whose parachutes had failed to open.

I realised that, given sufficient publicity in the Press on the Sunday, we might hear " something to our advantage," and I gave out the information. Fleet Street was delighted and took the opportunity. It was the lead story in every newspaper.

In view of the pathologist's statement about the possible use of an aeroplane, I directed that special inquiries be made at all airports and private airfields. Information came on Monday morning from Elstree aerodrome, Hertfordshire, to say that a man had hired a plane on October 5. Chief Inspector Jamieson went there immediately and discovered some amazing facts.

The aircraft had been chartered by a man named Hume, who had previously hired aircraft from there. He had paid £20 for a previous hiring in five-pound notes. (When Setty disappeared he had £1,000 in five-pound notes on him.)

Hume had arrived at the airfield in a motor-car, from which he took two bundles. They appeared to be heavy but he refused the attendants' offers of assistance and insisted

on placing the bundles into the aircraft himself. Mr.
Jamieson was told that one of the bundles measured about
two feet seven inches by two feet and was bulky.

Nothing further was heard of this particular plane that
day, but, on the morning of October 6, Hume arrived at
Elstree Airport again and stated that he had left the plane
at Southend Municipal Aerodrome owing to weather
conditions. He drove off in the car he had left at the airport
the previous day, went to Southend, placed another bundle
in the plane and took off, supposedly for Elstree. That was
soon after 4 p.m. on October 6.

Later that day, a message was received at Elstree from
Gravesend Air Control that the aeroplane hired by Hume
had landed there owing to weather conditions. Nothing
further was heard of Hume, and on October 10 the aeroplane was collected and flown back to Elstree, where it was
noticed that the port window had been damaged and the
front sliding portion had been jammed back and could not
be moved.

Further inquiries revealed that, on the evening of
October 5, Hume hired a car at Southend and was driven
to Golders Green. The fare was £4 5s. and he gave the
driver a five pound note. Again it was discovered that, on
October 6, he hired a car from Gravesend where the
aeroplane was abandoned and was driven to London.
Once again the driver was paid with a five-pound note.
All the facts were passed through to Superintendent
MacDougall, who made further inquiries in Essex.

The hunt was moving fast now, and the net closing. A
quick check on records elicited the fact that a Brian Donald
Hume lived at an address in Golders Green Road, and
accordingly, at 7 a.m. on October 26, Chief Inspector
Jamieson called there with Detective Inspector Evan Davies
and took him to Albany Street police station. He was told
that inquiries were being made in connection with the

murder of Stanley Setty and it was thought he might be able to assist. His reply was: " No, I can't help you with that. I know nothing about it." When asked to account for his movements on October 4 and 5, he quite properly replied that " it would be difficult." Later that day he was seen by Superintendent MacDougall and myself. When Mr. Mac-Dougall said to him: " I understand you hired an aeroplane on October fifth on to which you loaded two bundles and took off about five p.m." he shouted: " It's a lie. I put no parcels in the plane. All I had with me was my overcoat." He then hesitated, realising he had made an important admission.

Brian Hume was a good-looking young man, and cool. He had a natural ebullience and the most extraordinary self-confidence. It is a frightening thing to be taken to a police station when arrested for a major crime. I have seen the most arrogant individuals go to pieces in the C.I.D. office. There is an atmosphere at once friendly but clinical, a sureness in the way detectives move and talk, a feeling that they don't make many mistakes. Hume seemed to be singularly unworried. He sat in his chair and made a long, rambling statement.

He said that, on October 4, he was approached by three men who knew him as the " smuggling pilot." They asked him to dispose of some bundles by dropping them in the sea. He was to hire a plane for this work and would receive £150 for doing it. He agreed, and the men brought three bundles to his flat that night. The following day he went to Elstree and made arrangements about the plane.

The rest of his story agreed with what we already knew about placing two bundles on the plane and taking off for Southend. He spoke of pushing the bundles out opposite the pier and how difficult it was, of leaving the plane that night at Southend and dropping the third bundle next day, landing at Gravesend.

He admitted paying for the taxis, but said the money was given to him by the men for whom he had agreed to do the job. He agreed that he knew Setty and had done business with him in the past but denied seeing him on October 4.

From the time Hume had been taken from his flat two detectives had been there. There was nothing overtly suspicious but, when the flat was searched, a large, dark stain was seen on the underside of the carpet, which was established as human blood. The carpet had been taken for cleaning on October 5 and that blood-stain was therefore useless for grouping purposes. There were other traces of blood in the flat which were found to be Group O, the same as Setty's.

Another significant thing had happened on October 5. Hume took a large carving knife to a shop near his flat and had it sharpened. That knife was found in the flat. It was blunt then, but Dr. Camps said it could have been used to dismember the body. It was also significant that the fingerprint men searched every inch of that flat but could not find one print relating to Setty. And they had found none of Hume's on Setty's car.

Hume was charged with murder and also indicted as an accessory after the fact and, in January 1950, he was taken to the Old Bailey to stand his trial. He had been on remand in Brixton for several weeks, but appeared in the dock looking quite fresh and perfectly at ease.

The trial was remarkable for various reasons. For the first time after a jury had failed to agree, a new jury was sworn in, and without further evidence was directed to find Hume not guilty of murdering Stanley Setty. He pleaded guilty to being an accessory after the fact of murder, and the Director of Public Prosecutions, who was in court, took the decision to offer no evidence of murder when the second jury was sworn in.

Hume had faced three juries. The first was discharged

Donald Davidson, whom the
police sought for questioning

Agnes Walsh's snake-shaped
bracelet and watch

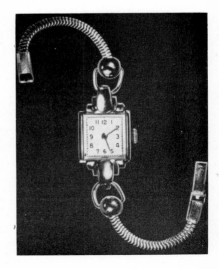

Lightning cartoonist Harry Michaelson, brutally murdered on Christmas night, 1948, for £5 8s. 9d.

The author relaxes with his
wife and daughter

when the judge was taken ill after one day's evidence. The second was re-sworn but failed to agree. To the third no evidence was offered on the charge of murder.

The closing day of the trial was dramatic. Hume had been down in the cells conferring with his brilliant counsel, Mr. R. F. Levy, Q.C. When he came back into court he was not so calm. To the jury the Clerk of the Court put the indictment charging Hume with Setty's murder. Mr. Christmas Humphreys, prosecuting, said simply: " Upon this indictment I offer no evidence."

In the next minute Hume pleaded guilty to the second charge, and Mr. Justice Sellers sentenced him to twelve years in gaol. In passing sentence he said: "I find it hard to imagine a case of a graver nature. For no other reason that we can see, other than for money—the sum of one hundred and fifty pounds—you were prepared to take part of a body and keep it in your flat overnight. And then, without any communication to the police, you took it away and put it in the Thames estuary with the intention and belief that nothing more would be known of it, thereby obliterating all evidence of murder."

Hume was one of the most brazen and hard-necked characters I met in all my service. He was an adventurer with a previous conviction for false pretences. He served for several months in the R.A.F., trained as a pilot and an air gunner and failed to qualify for either, and was eventually discharged as unfit. It was then that his vanity tempted him to dress himself as an R.A.F. pilot with wings and the ribbon of the D.F.M.

CHAPTER TWELVE

MURDER IN SUBURBIA

FIVE DAYS AFTER Stanley Setty was reported missing, on October 10, 1949, I decided to have an early night and to be home at ten p.m. I got there on time and in ten minutes was sitting down to a delightful mixed grill. Before I had finished, there was a ring on the front doorbell and in walked Inspector John Diller, the old friend whose wedding I had attended when I was at Vine Street. I offered him a drink, which, to my amazement, he refused.

" What's wrong, Jack? Given it up? " I asked.

" No, guv'nor. We've a double murder round the corner. I thought you'd like to know."

" Oh, yes," I said, " you've made my evening. I suppose one possible murder is not enough. Now you have to have two, and right on the doorstep."

Diller, I fancy, took slight umbrage at my remarks and murmured: " Anyway, I'm glad you had your dinner. Mine's still waiting."

I grinned, poured him a quick Scotch and we left in the car he had brought round. Diller told me that the bodies of a Mr. and Mrs. Goodman had been found. They had been battered to death with some heavy object and the house was in disorder. Apparently the Yard had been alerted at 10 p.m. by a 999 call, and Information Room had called the station. In that short time Diller had been busy. He had found out that the murdered couple were Jewish and that they had a young married daughter who had recently given birth to a child. The parents, together with their son-in-law, Daniel Raven, had, earlier that evening, been to visit their daughter, who was in a nursing home not far away at Muswell Hill. So far as he knew, they had only just returned when the murder took place.

" That looks as though this young Raven was the last person to see them if they came home together. Is he at the house? " I asked.

" No, he's not there, but I've sent round for him, so he should be there when we arrive."

I had been in the house but a few minutes when Chief Inspector Tansill came in. " This will teach you to give me tips on the Setty job," I said. " Now you've got one of your own."

The house was completely detached and spacious, surrounded by a beautiful garden. I went inside with Tansill and Diller and saw the most revolting sight in thirty years of service. Mr. and Mrs. Goodman had not merely been murdered—they had been butchered. Never before had I seen such violence.

Both bodies were lying on the floor of the living-room, with terrible head injuries. Mr. Goodman was in the middle of the room, his head towards the fireplace. He was completely dressed except for his jacket. On the table were his spectacles, and it looked to me as though he had been sitting at the table when the first blow was struck from behind. The lenses of his spectacles were spattered with blood. The middle of the solid mahogany table had a large indentation as though a heavy weapon had glanced off Goodman's head and smashed on to the table top. He had probably tried to rise and had then been hit again and fallen to the floor.

Mrs. Goodman was lying just inside the door with her head towards the centre of the room. She, too had severe head wounds, obviously caused by the same weapon. I noticed that the walls were splashed with blood but there seemed to be no evidence of any struggle. Those ferocious blows were struck from behind.

In the next room on the ground floor there was only one thing of note—a window was open. This window had an iron framework and opened outwards, an important clue because, to open the window without breaking it, the hand had to be on the inside. That window, then, was the means of escape only.

I went to the kitchen and there, lying in the sink, was the base of a television aerial which I later established as weighing two pounds eight and a half ounces. There was no doubt that it was the murder weapon. It fitted the indentation on the mahogany table exactly and an attempt had been made to wash it. In spite of that the blood had congealed and was visible.

Next I went upstairs to the bedrooms. In one, obviously that used by the dead couple, there was some disorder. A lady's coat and handbag were lying on the floor covered over by the quilt, which had been dragged off the bed. There was no money in the handbag but on the small table between the single beds there were six one-pound notes.

The open window on the ground floor, the rifled handbag and the disorder in the bedroom suggested a case of burglary, but the six one-pound notes would not have been ignored by a burglar who found time to rifle a handbag. It looked to me like a red herring being drawn over the trail. The question was, who and why?

I had just finished my examination when the son-in-law arrived. I told the detective to ask him to wait, because first I wanted to see Mr. Fraiman, Mrs. Goodman's brother, who was downstairs. It was he who had discovered the murders.

He was a pleasant and intelligent man. He was, he said, on friendly terms with the Goodmans and, in fact, interested in the electrical equipment business which Mr. Goodman ran in the West End of London.

I asked him to tell me briefly about the family. He said that the Goodmans' daughter, who was just twenty-one, had been married in June, 1948, to a young man called Daniel Raven and they lived nearby in a comfortable house given them by Mr. Goodman.

On October 6, four days previously, Mrs. Raven had given birth to a son and each evening her parents visited her in the nursing home a few miles away, usually accompanied by Raven. They returned home between 9.30 and 9.45 p.m. Knowing that, Mr. Fraiman, who also lived locally, called on the Goodmans each evening about 10 p.m. to get the latest news of the health of the new baby and its mother. On that evening Fraiman arrived, with his daughter, at 9.55 p.m. He noticed that the Goodmans' car was already in the garage and there was a light in the hall. He rang the bell and, when there was no reply, went round to the back and found a window open. He shouted but there was no answer, so he decided to investigate. He climbed through the open window and into the hall, and there, where the light was switched on, he saw the body of Mrs. Goodman.

Mr. Fraiman explained that the light switch in the living-room, where the bodies were, was on the woodwork near the floor behind the door. He walked in as carefully as possible, felt for the switch and then saw Mr. Goodman. He was still alive but unconscious and he died almost at once. Mr. Fraiman dialled 999 and then called the local doctor.

That was the second time that evening Mr. Fraiman had been at the Goodmans' house, for he had remained with the dead couple up to 7.50 p.m., when Mr. Goodman said he was going to make his usual visit to the nursing home.

I believed his story but, nevertheless, got Inspector

Diller to make a discreet call to the nursing home to check. A sister there confirmed it and said that the Goodmans, with Daniel Raven, had left shortly after 9 p.m. Diller also asked what clothes Raven was wearing.

I had lived in that district ever since being promoted to Chief Superintendent and knew exactly where the nursing home was, so I was fairly certain that the journey by car to the scene of the crime would have taken slightly more than twenty minutes and that the Goodmans had therefore arrived home at about 9.30 p.m.

As I write this, it seems perhaps as though that initial investigation took a long time. In fact it was all done in less than thirty minutes, which may seem surprising. The reason is that the experienced eye takes in many things quickly and enables one to draw preliminary conclusions.

Daniel Raven, meantime, had been in a room with some of the other relatives who had arrived at the house, and I was most anxious to see him separately. Accordingly, I directed Inspector Diller to take him to the police station. He protested, but was eventually taken there by Diller after I had spoken a few words to him. I was glad I had, for I noticed how clean his clothes looked, a trifle unusual at the end of a day. Diller whispered to me: " He's changed tonight."

It seemed that Diller had no sooner gone than he was back again, and excited. He told me that he had asked Raven for the keys to his house and Raven had resented it and was most annoyed when Diller said he intended going to the house. That was the kind of lead I was looking for, the first tangible clue brought about by Diller's sudden intuition and Raven's resentment. I went to his house at once, taking Tansill and Diller with me. When the front door opened we were hit in the face by a terrific smell of burning. We ran into the kitchen, the back door of which was open. In the stove was the gas poker, blazing, and something in the stove was well alight. Diller turned off the gas and carefully raked out the contents—a man's jacket and trousers. We carefully smothered the flames and stopped the smouldering. Here was a most important issue, and I decided to call out Detective Superintendent Cyril Cuthbert of the Forensic Laboratory. It was after midnight but he lived quite close and soon afterwards arrived with his chief, Dr. Holden. While they looked at the clothing we made a further search. We found a pair of blood-stained shoes in the garage and blood on the driving wheel, the hand brake and the front seat of Daniel Raven's car. The scientists were able to tell me that there were heavy patches of blood on the clothing removed from the boiler. Unfortunately, we were unable to find any other clothing such as a shirt or tie which could be connected with the circumstances of the night. But there were traces of blood in the kitchen sink and in the bath.

As we left the house a nearby clock struck one, and I decided that now was the time to see Raven. We drove to Edgware police station.

Raven was sitting in the C.I.D. office. He looked a pale, putty colour. I told him what had been found and asked him for an explanation. He was truculent and began to shout: " What right have you to question me? What power have you got to hold me here? None at all. Let me go." I asked again for an explanation, and he told me he would say nothing until he saw his solicitor. He arrived and advised his client to make a statement as to his movements that evening.

His statement merely said that he had been to the nursing home with Mr. and Mrs. Goodman and had travelled alone in his own car while the Goodmans went in their car. They left the nursing home a few minutes before he did, and when he got to their home they were already in the house. He went in for a few minutes and asked if he could stay the night, as he did not like being in his house alone. This request was refused and a few minutes later he left and went home. When he arrived there he put away his car and was preparing a bath for himself when he was told by Mr. Fraiman's daughter that there had been an accident at the Goodmans' house. He told the girl he would be there as soon as possible, put on the first thing that came to hand and hurried over. He admitted that the clothing in the boiler was his but added that he could not account for its being there.

It was not a long statement and told us nothing in the positive sense, but it was useful in that he chose not to explain many things. These first statements are often invaluable and very difficult to get round in the light of later discoveries.

I do not know whether Raven thought that his statement would be repaid by his being allowed to go home. If he did he was disappointed, for I ordered him to be detained.

At six o'clock in the morning I went home for a bath, shave and breakfast and then attended the post-mortem, which was conducted by Dr. Donald Teare. He revealed that Mr. Goodman had been hit on the head and face no less than fourteen times; his wife had been hit seven times. Dr. Teare had no doubt that the television aerial base was the murder weapon.

My next objective was to dispel the suggestion that robbery was the motive. It was painfully slender as it was, but murder investigation has to be exact. I had a careful search made of the house, this time in daylight, and in a safe under the stairs were many thousands of pounds in cash. The keys to that safe were in the trouser pocket of Mr. Goodman. In addition, there was jewellery and furs and odd sums of money which no expert burglar would have neglected.

Then there was the blood on Raven's clothing in the boiler, the blood on the shoes and in the motor car, all of which was analysed and found to be of the same group as the dead couple's.

There was another important point. At that time in October darkness fell soon after 6 p.m. When the Goodmans returned home they had obviously switched on the light in the living-room, for Mr. Goodman was sitting at the table with his jacket off. Yet when Mr. Fraiman found the bodies that light was off and the switch was in a place where no stranger would be likely to find it. In this connection there was one other important fact. There was an ordinary switch on the wall in the usual place by the door, but at that time it was disconnected through a fault. It was obviously necessary for the intruder to cover his crime with darkness and so ensure the maximum time between his crime and its discovery. Whoever it was, must have known where the lower light switch was or been unusually lucky in finding it.

Chief Inspector Tansill, Inspector Diller and myself held a short conference. All available detectives had been digging up what they could on the relationship between Raven and his father and mother-in-law and it seemed that there had been frequent quarrels. We reconstructed the crime as well as we were able, and it seemed that Raven, in a fit of temper, had grabbed the television aerial base, which stood outside the living-room door, and struck Mr. Goodman from behind while he was sitting at the table. Then he hit him again and again. Meantime, Mrs. Goodman, who had gone upstairs immediately upon arriving home, heard the noise, possibly her husband shouting, and ran downstairs. She too was struck first from behind, Raven being behind the door. Then she must have turned, for the rest of the blows were in her face and on the front of her head.

Now Raven was faced with two bodies in the room. He switched off the light and took the murder weapon into the kitchen to wash it. He knew that Mr. Fraiman would be calling in about thirty minutes. In order not to be suspected, he had simulated a burglary, but it was a poor effort. Then he had somehow to suggest the way the intruder had entered. He opened a window on the ground floor, climbed out and went home. He had made another mistake—he did not notice that the window opened only from the inside and there was no other way for an intruder to have entered. The rest of the house was securely locked.

We now had no doubts, and at 6 p.m. that day, twenty hours after the tragedy was discovered, Daniel Raven was charged with the double murder.

In the witness-box at the Old Bailey, he told his story of the events of that evening for the first time. He said that he drove back from the nursing home to the Goodmans' house and stepped into a pool of blood when switching on the light. That accounted for the blood on his clothing. Then he got frightened, panicked and drove home. He continued: " And the lies followed."

The importance of that first statement from Raven was now paramount. He stated that he had seen the Goodmans alive after returning from the nursing home, asked to stay the night, been refused, gone home and was preparing a bath when he heard the news.

The defence persisted that the murders were the work of some burglar and even suggested that Mr. Goodman had once given police information and that the crime was one of revenge.

Despite that, Raven was found guilty and sentenced to death. His appeal was dismissed and he was executed on January 6, 1950. Mr. Justice Cassels commended the officers in the case, in particular Inspector John Diller. It was, in fact, his case. He was first there and he tied Raven to the crime by first checking on his clothes and, secondly, getting the keys to the house and so stopping the destruction of the vital clue—the blood-stained jacket and trousers.

*　　*　　*

Agnes Walsh was a girl who had come to London from Ireland to find work. For a while she worked as a waitress in small cafés and in one or two dubious clubs, making a meagre living. And then, when she was only twenty years old, she decided to join the more lucrative ranks of the street girls and began to hang around Piccadilly Circus, looking for clients. She had no difficulty in finding them, and, if they were sufficiently generous, she knew of one or two small hotels in the Paddington area where she could take them.

There was a time when the " square mile of vice," as it is called—the area from Charing Cross Road to Park Lane bounded by Piccadilly on one side and Oxford Street on the other—was an accurate description. Now this vice trade has spilled over into other parts of London, particularly Paddington, which, in 1950, was my headquarters. It is on the fringe of that square mile.

Until Derby Day, May 27, 1950, I had never heard of Agnes Walsh, but I saw her at eleven that morning. She was dead. An hour before, the chambermaid in a boarding house in Sussex Gardens, Paddington, was cleaning up the rooms. She was used to finding the rooms empty, for the boarding house catered mostly for people who wished to stay only one night. The door to Room 12 opened easily enough and the chambermaid took one look, turned and ran. On the bed was a naked woman and round her neck was tied a nylon stocking. The manager of the boarding house called Paddington, and I was telephoned at Albany Street, where I was in discussion with Inspector John Gosling. We jumped into a car and drove straight to this wide tree-lined road with its contrasting houses, some hand-some, some faded and dilapidated.

It was clear that this murder was no secret. Already, the crime reporters and their photographers were there in force—I counted about forty of them. The flashlight bulbs exploded all round as we got out of the car, which prompted John Gosling, an irrepressible humorist, to remark: " Looks like the Blackpool illuminations." I climbed the stairs and found Inspector Evan Davies there with his sergeant, and the Yard photographers and fingerprint men. The room was sparsely furnished and I could detect the slightly musty odour of the boarding house. There was a plain wash-hand stand, an ordinary wooden double bed on which lay the body of the dead girl.

There had obviously been a fierce struggle. The bed-clothes were all over the room and the carpet had been kicked up. There were blood marks on the wall at the foot of the bed and near the wash basin. On the carpet I found some hairs. Hanging over a chair, on which the dead girl's underclothes were neatly piled, was a nylon stocking. The other was tied tightly round her neck.

I remember well that it was a beautiful sunny day when life seemed good and all the trees along Sussex Gardens were in bloom. I looked out of the dusty window and thought that this was an awful end to the life of a young girl. She had just had her twenty-second birthday.

Dr. Francis Camps, the pathologist, who had been called earlier, arrived and started his examination. He confirmed that the girl had been strangled and had been dead several hours. He fixed the time of the attack at between five-forty-five and seven-forty-five that morning. He was also able to tell me that the girl had probably fought for her life, for she had received six blows on her face consistent with heavy fist punches. Two of the blows caused deeper wounds, and he suggested that the murderer probably wore a ring of some kind. In his opinion, the nylon stocking was put round the neck after death and he found that a green-bordered handkerchief was in her mouth, pressed firmly into the back of the throat.

He examined the girl's hands and arms and found some scratches there. From his bag he took some envelopes and a nail file and carefully scraped underneath her finger-nails, catching the fragments in the small envelopes. Since there had been a fight it was possible that, secreted under her fingernails, were particles of the murderer's skin or materials from his clothes. The fight also presupposed that the murderer himself was marked on the face and hands.

The girl's handbag did not seem to have been interfered with and it contained correspondence addressed to Agnes Walsh. Nevertheless, to make absolutely sure of identity, I asked one of the detectives to take her fingerprints, which were sent to the Yard. In the meantime, Inspector Davies had called C.R.O. to see if anything was known in the name of Agnes Walsh. The reply came at once: Convictions for prostitution, frequents Piccadilly area, born 1928, sister resides in Mornington Crescent, Camden Town, also a prostitute.

The murderer seemed to have left no clues and I called for the manager of the house to bring me the register. He was able to account for all the residents except a couple who had signed in as " Mr. and Mrs. Davidson," which was followed by an almost indecipherable address. It was likely that " Mrs. Davidson " was the dead woman and " Mr. Davidson " the murderer. The manager remembered the couple arriving. He was quite sure it was the same woman and he was able to give a fairly good description of the man.

I sent a detective with a car to bring the dead girl's sister, Margaret, to the station. She, too, was pretty and spoke with a broad Irish accent. She said she was with Agnes in

Piccadilly the previous evening and had seen her talking to a man who was a complete stranger. She was unable to give much of a description but she did tell me that her sister always wore a cocktail watch on a snake bracelet, and two rings. All those articles were missing. It looked to me as if the murderer wanted to make us think that robbery was the motive, but since he had not touched the handbag I surmised that here was the normal red herring.

I had a sketch made of a similar watch and gave it to the Press with a rough description of the man. Then I sent my detectives to Piccadilly to locate some of the other girls to try to pick up an accurate description of the wanted man. It is an established fact in police work that people generally are not keen observers and their ideas of describing a person vary as wildly as the English climate. The few things these witnesses agreed on was that the man was softly spoken, sad-faced and that he had an accent.

That description, meagre though it was, was passed to the Yard for circulation. Added to it was this important piece of information: " May be badly scratched on face, neck, hands or arms." Within a few seconds, that message was being teleprinted to all main stations in London and printed in the *Police Gazette*, which is circulated throughout the country, together with the sketch of the watch on the snake bracelet.

That sketch was also printed in the Pawn List which is circulated by police to pawnbrokers and jewellers. There was just a chance the murderer might try to sell the watch.

Meanwhile, the visitors' register was subjected to some very close scrutiny, and from the badly written address we managed to decipher the words " Co. Durham," or at least so it seemed.

Later that day Chief Inspector Jamieson, who had been at Epsom for Derby Day duty, returned and took charge of the inquiry. With Inspector Davies and other detectives he combed the West End throughout the evening, for it was reasonable to assume that the wanted man was still in London. There are few better places in the world to hide.

Day after day, night after night, the relentless search went on, but there was still no trace of the wanted man. I was beginning to think he had succeeded in getting away from London. Neither was there any trace of the missing jewellery at the various pawnbrokers or anywhere else. Then, suddenly, I received a police telegram from Houghton-le-Spring, County Durham. (I had previously asked them to make inquiries for a man called Davidson.) The telegram said that a local family reported that their son, Donald Davidson, had disappeared from home wearing white baker's clothes and a sports jacket. He had driven off in his sports car that morning and not been seen since.

The man's description and that of the car were circulated to the police of the surrounding counties. The net was closing in and I was sure that this was the right man. It was the same name, the same county. I was even more sure when the Durham police told me that they understood he had driven with a friend to London for the Derby.

It was impossible for Davidson to get far. Every police force in the country was alerted and a watch kept on all main roads.

That morning, the daily papers had carried the news that Scotland Yard officers were making inquiries in Durham to trace the man responsible for the murder of Agnes Walsh. It was the first time that news had been published and it looked as though Davidson had read the papers when he was up early working in the family bakery and had decided to leave. Within a few hours the hunt was over. Davidson was found shot dead near picturesque Finchley Priory, only a few miles from his home.

In those peaceful surroundings, far from the busy

Metropolis where he had succumbed to a momentary savage impulse, he ended his life at the age of twenty-nine.

I sent Chief Inspector Jamieson and Detective Inspector Davies up to Davidson's home to continue their inquiries and to interview the friend with whom he had been in London on holiday, and to search for the missing jewellery. The hunt was really over, but there was still the coroner's inquest to inquire into the cause of the death of Agnes Walsh, and if possible establish the identity of the person who had caused her death.

Davidson, it appeared, had left his home with a friend to go on a fortnight's motoring holiday. They drove to Liverpool, then south to Torquay and Bournemouth, reaching London on May 25, when they booked into an hotel at Euston. On that evening they went out and about seeing the sights together but, on the Friday evening, the 26th, Davidson went out alone. The next morning, while Agnes Walsh was lying dead, he returned to his hotel, and his friend saw that he was badly scratched about the face and hands, that his clothes were untidy and he was very agitated. Davidson explained to his friend that he had been involved in a drunken brawl and appeared disinclined to talk further.

It had been Davidson's intention to go to Epsom to see the Derby run, but later in the morning he decided that the injuries to his face were too bad. He obviously thought he might be recognised so decided to stay in the hotel.

During the day, however, he sent out several times for newspapers making believe that it was the horse-racing he was interested in, but what he read there must have panicked him, for that evening he insisted that they should drive back home through the night. They set off early in the evening.

For the next few days, until his flight, he worked away as usual in his parents' bakery business, but his misery would

The Information Room at New Scotland Yard

River Police motor launch patrols the Thames

Chief Supt. Beveridge (r.) with Supt. J. Jamieson (l.) and Sergt. Pierce Butler on the Michaelson case

Left (in uniform): Sir Norman Kendal, then Assistant Commissioner, with Mr. John Horwell, Chief Constable C.I.D., at a police inspection in Hyde Park in 1935. The author is seen left, marked with a cross

At a police inspection by Her Majesty in Hyde Park, 1954. *Left to right:* Detective Chief Supt. T. Barratt, the author, Detective Supt. C. Sparks, Detective Chief Supt. E. Greeno, and Detective Chief Supt. W. Chapman

be easy to imagine. He had a loving mother and father and, until this time, had been a devoted son. Now he was tormented with fear of arrest, fear of his parents' heartbreak, and fear of bringing disgrace on the family name. So he went on the run, obviously with a fixed idea in mind—to end it all.

Having come to the empty caravan in this very desolate spot, he decided that here was the ideal place for his purpose. He set to work swiftly to seal the caravan and then turned on the tiny gas stove. He was not to know, however, that the gas was in fact non-poisonous but highly inflammable. Shortly afterwards, for some reason or other, there was a terrific explosion and Davidson was flung through the doorway into the field. He was badly burned and bleeding and, as he staggered about, fell into some nearby bushes. Then there was a single pistol shot which, for the second time that morning, disturbed the peaceful glade, and all was quiet.

I never found out what happened to the cocktail watch with the snake bracelet or the two rings. Neither was it ever established why the murder happened at all. It was the general assumption that something that the girl had done had upset Davidson who, being in drink, went mad.

The information my officers obtained suggested that Davidson was generally a very quiet young man who drank little, but he had a quick temper, which supported my theory.

At the coroner's inquest into the cause of death, the jury returned a verdict of murder against some person or persons unknown. Davidson himself might, by his action, have escaped publicity, but unfortunately his family did not, because the whole of the evidence had to be gone into, and I felt desperately sorry for them.

You might think that the evidence appeared very black against Davidson, and so it was. And you might therefore wonder at the verdict. In the circumstances, I think it was the only one possible in the absence of actual proof, but, had Davidson lived and the police caught up with him, I think the position would have been different. I have no doubt whatever that the necessary evidence would have been forthcoming to clinch the matter but, as it was, the verdict must remain.

At the inquest, Chief Inspector Jamieson was asked: " If you had come across Davidson and he had been alive, what would you have done? " He replied, simply: " I would have apprehended him and brought him back to London on a charge of murder."

CHAPTER THIRTEEN

DEATH FOR CHRISTMAS

JUST BEFORE CHRISTMAS, 1948, I was invited to Elliot House, in Paddington, the local section house, to see a variety show. Every month or so, these stag parties were held and all the famous stars in London came along to perform. One of the artists that night was Harry Saul Michaelson, known as " One Minute Michaelson," a lightning cartoonist. He had appeared many times on the stage and on television and I thoroughly enjoyed his show. Afterwards I was introduced to him and we talked for a few minutes. The next time I saw him he was dead, cruelly murdered in his own flat.

It was a few days later, on Boxing Day, and I was sitting at home in the late evening when the telephone rang and I was told by one of my officers at Paddington that a man had been attacked in his flat and was not expected to live. I was told that Mr. Jamieson was already there and had asked that I be informed.

I went at once. I knew exactly where it was, just behind busy Baker Street in one of the better residential areas of Paddington very near to Mayfair.

A car arrived, with Scobbie at the wheel, and I went off just before midnight to try and probe yet another murder.

When I arrived at the block of flats I could hear the sounds of revelry, music, gay laughter, singing. I stood for a moment in the empty street and looked around. Fairy lights twinkled in all the windows and, faintly, I could hear the clink of glasses. Then I turned and walked into the block of flats. The policeman on guard at the door saluted. " First door on the right, sir."

Chief Inspector Jamieson was there, a tall, lean, smartly dressed figure in a dark coat and Homburg hat. " Hallo, guv'nor," he said. " Happy Christmas." His tone was understandably sour.

" Who is it? " I asked.

" The fellow we met the other night, Harry Michaelson. Looks as though someone got in and was surprised."

Jamieson, a veteran of murder investigation, had wasted no time. He told me that the porter of the flats had heard screaming about midnight and come out of his quarters to see what was wrong. He had found Michaelson standing at his flat door bleeding from a severe wound on the temple. He dialled 999 and the crew of the radio car rushed the victim off to St. Mary's Hospital, where he died shortly after arrival.

The porter was able to help further. He told us that Mrs. Michaelson, the dead man's wife, was out of London and that he had been staying in the flat alone.

" I've sent for Fred Cherrill (the Superintendent in charge of fingerprints)," said Jamieson. " I fancy *that*." He pointed to a tubular steel chair, which was lying on its side and in it a slight dent. There were blood-stains on the legs.

It was a nice room, furnished in exquisite taste, but now in a shambles. Chairs and tables were overturned, lamps upset, the carpet pushed up and ornaments knocked on the floor. There were splashes of blood here and there. It was clear that Michaelson had been in bed when the intruder entered. There was an open window, easily reached from the street, and it looked as though the murderer had come in that way. Michaelson had perhaps been aroused by some noise, possibly the burglar falling over some article of furniture, and had wakened, turned on the light and challenged the intruder.

The dead man's trousers were lying on the floor at the foot

of the bed and his jacket was still around the chair which had also been overturned.

Mr. Jamieson searched all the pockets but there was no money. It looked as though this was the motive—robbery.

Inspector Evan Davies (now a superintendent) walked in. " He died without saying anything," he said. He was referring to the fact that two detectives had sat by Michaelson's bedside just in case he could give any clue to his attacker. Davies went on: " I have all the boys working the district and all the stations to see if they can pick up anybody."

A message had already gone to the Information Room and to all stations giving brief particulars of the murder with instructions that the clothing of all suspects should be examined for blood-stains. Many an innocent person was stopped that night, swiftly interrogated and, after a suitable apology, allowed to go. These " stops," as they are called, may be a slight nuisance but they are necessary and, quite often, most effective.

We were faced with the most difficult of all murders. There was no history of association with the dead man, no description, and it appeared that the visitor had stolen only cash, which was unidentifiable. It was fairly certain the wanted man was a housebreaker or burglar of a violent disposition, and that was the most we could say. But we had one chance.

I was convinced that Chief Inspector Jamieson was right in his deduction that the tubular steel chair was the murder weapon, and when Chief Superintendent Cherrill took it away for expert examination at his office at the Yard I was fairly sure he would find some kind of useful fingerprint. In fact, he did find one single print impression which, as it turned out, proved invaluable.

At that time it didn't help us very much. Single print impressions take a long time to search. They involve an enormous amount of checking and comparison, and if the mark is on record it may be one of millions. In the Finger-print Department at the Yard there are many experts who spend their entire time trying to track down single prints. In recent history there was the case of the Potters Bar murder when these single-print experts went through many thousand palm prints before they found the one they wanted.

That we had to leave for the experts, and meanwhile we carried on with our local inquiries. Detectives went to flats all over the area, where everybody was still in party mood. People interviewed thought we were joking when told that a murder had been committed nearby. They refused to be serious, and asked the detectives in for a drink. It was clear from all of these flats that nobody had heard anything, and we could expect no help from them.

We traced Michaelson's movements throughout that day and discovered that he had entered his flat at about 8 p.m. and had not been seen again until he was found standing at his door bleeding from the head. The flat was about three feet below ground level with a fairly spacious area surrounded by iron railings. The main doors of the block were barred at midnight and remained closed unless opened for latecomers by the night porter. Apart from the one room the flat appeared to be intact, and when Mrs. Michaelson returned home she confirmed this. She estimated that her husband would have had something like £5 in cash in his possession, but no cash was found in the flat of any kind.

Mrs. Michaelson supplied us with the names and addresses of various friends of her husband and herself, and all of these were asked whether they had seen the dead man on Christmas Day or Boxing Day, but none of them could help in any way. Day after day the search went on in the underworld to find this mysterious intruder. There had been several small cases of local flatbreaking since the murder and, one night, talking to Chief Inspector Jamieson, I suggested that the man might be fool enough to remain in the district and continue his activities. It seemed a far-fetched suggestion at the time but, if that were so, I reasoned that he was probably a complete stranger to London.

Chief Inspector Jamieson got together his " Aids to C.I.D.," all young and enthusiastic men who cared not how many hours they worked. He told them what we thought and stressed the enormous importance of the job they were about to do. He said: " Get on to the ground; work all the hours that God sends; and you must catch this murderer. The chances are that he comes from the country, so look twice at anyone with an accent."

These young fellows patrolled every day, every night, until dawn and, on January 19, just over three weeks after the murder, two young policemen saw a man acting suspiciously in the St. John's Wood area of Marylebone, and arrested him as a suspect. He had no fixed address and declined any information about himself. He was interviewed about his movements around Christmas, without of course mentioning the murder, but he proved vague and said nothing very helpful. As in all arrests, his fingerprints were taken and sent up to the Yard. The following morning I was in my office when Chief Superintendent Cherrill phoned me from Scotland Yard and said: " Peter, this man charged as a suspect in St. John's Wood may be the man you want for your Boxing Day murder. I think you'd better get along to see him."

I called on Chief Inspector Jamieson and Detective Inspector Evan Davies, and we went to see this suspect, whose name was Harry Lewis. He was in one of the cells at Marylebone magistrates' court waiting to appear on the suspect charge. He was only twenty-one, slim and dark and roughly dressed.

I was there for a short time while he was being interrogated, and after Lewis had got over the initial shock of
being challenged with the murder, and wondering how on
earth we had caught up with him, he admitted that he was
the person who had entered the flat to steal whatever he
could. He had awakened the man asleep in bed. When
the man got up to remonstrate with him, he had struck him
on the head with the chair, knocked him to the floor and
then run away.

Later on he made a full statement. He described how he
had been wandering around with no money. He got in
through the open window and was in the act of taking
money from Michaelson's trouser pocket when he was
challenged. Lewis struck him several times on the head
and body with the chair and then ran into the street. We
secured more evidence from his clothes, which, when
examined at the laboratory, were found to be blood-stained.

Lewis appeared at Marylebone magistrates' court and
refused legal aid, but later changed his mind and was
given a solicitor. Many weeks later, he arrived at the Old
Bailey and was found guilty and sentenced to death. He
had no defence whatsoever. He had decided to break in and
steal what he could, was unfortunately surprised, and instead
of just running away had panicked and become violent.
Later he appealed before Mr. Justice Hilbery, Mr. Justice
Birkett and Mr. Justice Finnemore, but his plea was dismissed and he was hanged in Pentonville Gaol.

This case may again illustrate how amazingly useful are
the back-room boys of Scotland Yard—in this case the
men in the Fingerprint Department. He had left a single
fingerprint, but they are hard to identify. He had a record,
although he was a young man, and if he had left more
evidence of his fingers he might have been readily identified.
Even so, he was a Welshman, a stranger in London, and

would have been hard to locate. Here was a case of perseverance by two young C.I.D. aspirants, in picking up the man in the same area as the murder was committed, and of the patience and skill of the fingerprint men at the Yard. Once again it proved the efficacy of keeping single finger-prints separate and comparing them with any new set which came in. In this case, when Lewis's fingerprints were sent to the Yard a general search was made and his record found. Then the form was sent to the Scenes of Crime section, where they had the record left on the steel chair, the murder weapon. The comparison was exact—the case was solved.

This was in fact a murder committed for £5 8s. 9d. I am pretty sure, having met Mr. Michaelson who was a kindly man, that if Lewis, especially at Christmastime, had asked his victim for some money he would have got it. If that had happened, both these men might have been alive today.

POSTSCRIPT

A DETECTIVE'S DAY has no end, especially in the early stages. As I climbed the promotion ladder the work was more interesting but still endless. In my final rank, that of Chief Superintendent, the days were the most exciting of my service. Looking at the crime scene in my area was like studying a giant jigsaw puzzle. Every Division and every station had its own problems, and my job was to advise and direct my staff and, wherever necessary, take over the investigation myself. The morning report, which was on my desk at 9.30 a.m., sometimes contained practically every crime in the calendar; there might be a murder, rape, arson, housebreaking and countless different types of theft. When I looked at those reports, I knew that one of my detectives was working on every case and that they would go on working.

Later, the detectives, if they were successful, would send me their final report which contained all the evidence against the accused person plus their complete background. The next stage was to bring the prisoner to court, where all the evidence collected was given before the magistrate or judge. Quite often I would sit in the courts and watch my men give their evidence and see them attacked by the lawyer for the defence. Giving evidence is an art, and there is hardly a detective I have ever known who does not approach that witness-box without a slight twinge of nervousness. It is rather like an actor on a first night, but in the police there are too many first nights.

In my thirty-five years of service I must have stood in the

box many hundreds of times. Sometimes the case went quietly, sometimes violently. I remember one particular case during the war when I had charged a jeweller and his son with receiving stolen property. Their shop was in a yard in Whitechapel, known locally as " Aladdin's Alley " because nearly all the shops there sold expensive jewellery. It was said to be the richest street in the East End of London. It was quite an ordinary case in its way—the men were charged with receiving about £1,000 worth of jewellery—but the trial at the Old Bailey was sensational in that the defence counsel made a strong attack on the police evidence which included some unpleasant allegations as to the honesty of my detectives.

The case lasted four days and each day the newspaper headlines grew bigger. On the final day the judge decided to sit later than the usual four o'clock, and soon afterwards the jury retired to consider their verdict. They returned to find the prisoners guilty and I then mounted the steps of the box to give evidence of the background of the men in the dock. I had just finished when every light in the court went out. I stood still and then saw an amazing scene. It was the time of the blackout and most people were carrying torches, which they switched on, making crossbeams that looked like searchlights in the sky. Everyone seemed to be shouting and I could see that the prison officers had moved closer to the prisoners in the dock. Then, suddenly, I heard the quiet, measured tones of the Recorder, Sir Gerald Dodson, who said he would defer judgment until the following morning. As he completed his sentence and was rising from his chair, a voice called out: " This is the sort of justice you get here—Black Justice! "

All the papers carried even bigger headlines next morning, but the mystery of the lights was cleared up when the judge opened the court. The chief engineer explained that the lights were switched off each day at four o'clock to ensure complete blackout and he was unaware that the court was still in session.

There were some exciting cases, of course, that never went to court, particularly the capture of escaped prisoners. I suppose John Edward Allen, the " Mad Parson," had as much publicity as any man after he had climbed over the wall of Broadmoor Criminal Lunatic Asylum one night. He was a child-murderer and a leading light in the " The Broadhumorists," as the inmates called their concert party. When he escaped he took with him some of the theatrical properties, including a waiter's suit and a parson's collar and jacket. He was on the run for twenty-one months and then was found in a room less than three hundred yards from one of my police stations!

One evening, the C.I.D. at Southwark received a tip from a baker that he was sure Allen was working for him in an assumed name and was living in Albany Street, near Regent's Park. Sergeant Sidney Ray at Albany Street police station took the call from Southwark and was not over-enthusiastic. He, like every other detective in the Force, had received hundreds of calls from people who were convinced they had seen Allen, but he went along just the same. In one corner of the room were a couple of canaries, singing happily. The man in bed laughed convincingly when Sergeant Ray challenged him, and for a moment he thought that this was just another false tip. Then he caught sight of the man in profile and noticed that one ear-lobe was much lower than the other, which was a major point in the *Police Gazette*. Ray didn't challenge any more but said: " Come on, Allen, I know it's you. Get dressed."

Allen, looking perfectly composed, grinned and asked for Ray's pocket-book in which he wrote: " John Edward Allen, the ' Mad Parson,' " and then meekly walked to the station, the blue light of which he could see from the window of his room!

That report came to my desk in the morning in these brief words: " Arrested: John Edward Allen."

At least once every week I attended a senior officers' conference at the Yard, which was presided over by the Assistant Commissioner for Crime. For the greater part of my service that post was held by Sir Norman Kendal, an amazing man with a wealth of knowledge about criminals and the most extraordinary affection for the C.I.D. At those conferences we would discuss the current trends of crime, suggest methods to stop certain new ideas and generally keep on top of the underworld. We did not always succeed; there were times when the criminals were on top, but not for long.

The so-called gangsters occasionally gave trouble. They had their gangs of strong-arm men who walked around armed with razors or coshes and sometimes guns, and one night there was a clash between two of the main London gangs. One of a King's Cross crowd received serious knife injuries and was detained in hospital. He refused to talk, but my colleague in the next district, Chief Superintendent Tom Barratt, asked one of the gang leaders to go to the West End Central police station for a chat.

I had heard that the same gangs were planning to resume their fight at Harringay Arena on the night of the Baksi *v.* Woodcock fight, so I also went along to see the leader. I had never met him before but he had a tough reputation and I expected a battle, at least of words. Instead he was very meek and mild and accepted my hint that I would view any trouble at Harringay in a very personal way. He made only one point—that I tell the other gang the same thing. I agreed to that, an easy decision because I intended to let them know of my interest in them anyway. Despite these moves I took full precautions on the night of the fight but there was no sign of either of the rival gangs, and the only person who got hurt that night was Woodcock—at the hands of Baksi!

That was one of the little things that did not get recorded, one of the odd items that are part of the policeman's lot and which come under the heading of " prevention of crime," a primary object of police work. They are part of the general day, which includes an endless variety of criminal patterns.

When I began, the weekly wage was £3 10s. and that had been brought about by the famous police strike of 1919 after which many hundreds of policemen lost their jobs. Before that a constable was expected to exist on about 32s. 6d. a week, to remain efficient and to resist the temptation of corruption. There are countless members of the underworld who seek to destroy your good name; crooked men and women who spend their lives hating the police and who care nothing for fair play but will use any dirty trick and subterfuge to remove a detective who is too efficient.

Set against that is the magnificent *esprit de corps* of the Force and the fascination of man-hunting which gets into the blood and makes other pursuits dull by comparison. There is a certain amount of danger and bursts of tremendous excitement, the nerve-tingling thrill of the chase and the satisfaction of a capture. It is a battle of wits with the dice loaded slightly in your favour. If you win the battle, the criminal goes to prison. What is the reward of the detective? The satisfaction of a job well done, a possible commendation and a growing reputation. It certainly does not mean accelerated promotion as described so often in works of fiction.

In my years I have seen many changes, particularly in criminals. I have arrested hundreds of men and women, and even some children. I have investigated crimes against both rich and poor. I saw the gangs form and fight on the racecourses.

I watched the C.I.D. grow from a few hundred men to its present size of more than 1,500. I saw the advent of the women police, the growth of the Flying Squad and the Fraud Squad. In those years criminals have changed their tactics and have become more cunning as the C.I.D. have improved their methods. I remember when the smash-and-grab raids began, and when the safe-blowers started up in business.

In my thirty-five years the police have become a streamlined force equipped to fight succeeding new generations of more skilful thieves and murderers.

There were few cars when I started and no 999 system. There was no scientific laboratory as we know it now. Everything moved more slowly and the policeman's job was, in some ways, more difficult. He was the master of his beat, friend to the majority and foe of the few.

In one area there are the houses of the wealthy in Mayfair. Here also are hundreds of elegant, well-stocked shops, the prey of the women shoplifters, known to the underworld as " hoisters."

The West End criminals were delighted when in September, 1940, the new West End Central police station was bombed. I was chief of the Flying Squad then, and that night I went to the station to discuss the problem of looting with the late Chief Superintendent Arthur Thorp, who was then the Divisional Detective Inspector. The discussion over, I went with some other officers to a local hostelry for a drink and a snack. I left my Squad car outside the station, having told the driver and the wireless operator to wait in the station as the air-raid warning had sounded.

Less than two minutes after ordering our food there was a terrific explosion and the basement room bar came in on top of us. We were unhurt and managed to stagger up the stairs to the street. The Squad car had disappeared and the street looked like Ypres in the first world war.

We ran to the station and learned that a large bomb had been parachuted on to the building opposite the station. There were twenty-six police casualties, including Mr. Thorp, who was badly wounded about the head and body by flying glass. I looked around but could not find him. Many hours later, I tracked him down in another police station, smothered in bandages but as chirpy as ever.

I remember some other gentry in the West End who tried to make life difficult. They were the mock-auction crowd who took shops in Oxford Street and were making a lot of money. Their racket was, and still is, to put up inferior goods for auction at ridiculously low prices and to induce the customers to believe they can get " something for nothing." The fast, smooth-talking auctioneer having secured the attention of his crowd and mesmerised them into a receptive frame of mind, holds up a sealed box. " Who will offer me five pounds for this box without knowing what is in it? I can see you are sporting people. I've played fair by you, so who will give me a bid? " Invariably a " mug " takes a chance and finds he has bought some worthless trinket. He complains and is talked out of it by the auctioneer and his many helpers, and, in the end, is glad to escape from the shop alive. It was difficult to prosecute, for the victims seldom had very clear memories and did not want to become involved in unpleasant publicity.

I stopped this racket, but one morning a man who refused to give his name telephoned me: " You are slipping, Mr. Beveridge; the mock-auction mob are back in business." A quick check confirmed his news and I again began planting my men in the crowd, making it difficult for the mobs to operate. They actually persuaded their solicitors to write to the Yard, complaining! That meant that I had to make a detailed and official report. I was backed to the hilt by my superiors and within a few days the mock-auction mob was forced away from the West End. I had the great satisfaction one day of picking up the telephone to hear a mouthful of ripe invective from one of the fake Auctioneers. I was extremely flattered.

Some months ago, when I retired, I said in a broadcast on " In Town Tonight " that, if I had to begin life again, I would still choose the police force. I am still of the same opinion. I was one of the lucky ones and reached the rank of Chief Superintendent. I gladly endured the long hours and the inevitable frustrations of jobs that went wrong but, most of all, I enjoyed the good fellowship of my colleagues. To their loyalty and team-spirit I can only pay an inadequate tribute. The reader will judge from these random recollections how very great a part they played in so many of the cases in which I gained the limelight of publicity.

I would like finally to pay tribute to my wife for her unfailing patience and understanding during all the years when she knew not when to expect me home and for her many kind words of advice at the criticial moments in my career; and to my daughter Margaret whom I sometimes had to neglect when working for weeks in London and elsewhere. This is part of the price that every police officer has to pay, from the humble man on the beat to his superiors in the highest ranks of Scotland Yard.

APPENDIX

THE FOLLOWING EXTRACTS are taken from the Report of Her Majesty's Inspectors of Constabulary for the year ended 30th September, 1955 (published by Her Majesty's Stationery Office). In the light of the Author's observations on the changes and development of the Police Force in his thirty-five years of duty, the official summary at the close of the inspection year when he retired may help to supplement and perhaps underline his personal views.

" At the close of the inspection year (30th September, 1955) the authorised establishments had risen to 53,647, a total increase of 750. The strength dropped to 47,992, making a deficit of 5,655, so that the available strength of regular policemen was 419 less than at the end of the previous year. The actual strength includes men undergoing basic training and in various stages of the probationary period of two years. In addition, 207 constables of the first police reserve were employed wholetime.

" Duties have been reviewed and where necessary reorganised. Improved mobility has enabled some beats to be extended, and this has been done either by providing a light-weight motorcycle or small car, or by granting a mileage allowance for a privately owned motor-cycle or small car. More important still has been the progressive replacement of police officers on indoor duties where police training and experience or the authority of a constable are not necessary by men and women with clerical or tradesmen's qualifications, with scales of pay and conditions of employment appropriate to the tasks. Progress was also made in a number of forces with the reorganisation of ranks and responsibilities, particularly by making provision in the establishments of larger

194

forces for the responsibilities discharged by the senior officers to be recognised by appropriate upgrading of rank.

" The inability of many police authorities to recruit, and to retain, adequate numbers of police makes it impracticable for us to press them to consider such increases in their establishments as might otherwise be urged if conditions were normal. By reason of the growth of urban communities and other developments, and the greater traffic densities on many roads, the wide gaps between establishment and strength which persist in many forces are a cause for anxiety which would be greater but for the fact that the organisation, training and efficiency of the police have so greatly improved.

" At the beginning of the inspection year the number of vacancies for men stood at 4,486, and at the close had risen to 5,655. This was 1,169 more than at the start of the year, inclusive of the additional vacancies by augmentations to establishments. A total of 3,488 men were appointed on probation, but against this intake 3,953 men left the service. In the previous year 3,502 joined and 3,268 left. Of the wastage during the year, 915 were probationers (850), 1,188 others resigned before qualifying for pension or gratuity (858), 1,746 were pensioned on completion of service or on grounds of ill-health (1,453), and 104 left for other reasons or died in the service (107). The figures given in brackets are the corresponding totals for the previous year.

" The loss by resignation in the year of over 2,000 men before they qualified for pension was the heaviest drain of its kind for some years, and we made it our duty in the course of inspections to examine in detail the individual reasons given by men for leaving the service. We found that the losses of the greater proportion were fairly evenly divided amongst the following reasons:

(*a*)   To obtain more remunerative employment;
(*b*)   Inability to settle down to the life and duties (including discipline, varying shift or split duties);
(*c*)   Domestic difficulties, particularly where wives are unwilling to face up to the varying hours which police duty

involves for their husbands on bank holidays, in the evenings, at weekends, and in all weathers.

(*d*)   Emigration, including appointment to a Commonwealth or Colonial police force.

" Youths engaged primarily for their potential fitness as constables are now employed in the majority of police forces. More recently it has become the practice to designate them as cadets, and marked success has followed their employment on suitable duties in police stations and headquarters offices. Concurrently with this employment a programme of pre-service training is arranged in most forces, designed to improve the fitness of cadets for eventual appointment as constables. A cadet branch, in providing a steady flow of a proportion of the recruits needed for the force, has the great advantage of offering a police career to suitable boys at school-leaving age. Pre-service training as a cadet allows more time for assessing potential fitness for the office of constable.

" During the year under review 27 inspectors and 186 sergeants from county, city and borough police forces (including the City of London) completed junior courses at the Police College, and 67 inspectors and 18 chief inspectors from similar forces completed their attendance at senior courses. In addition, one woman inspector attended the senior and four women sergeants attended junior courses. These figures bring the total number of officers (men and women) from the above-mentioned forces who, since the College was established in 1948, have attended one of the two main courses to 1,641 for the junior and 611 for the senior course.

" Twenty-seven superintendents and chief superintendents attended the College for short courses of three weeks' duration to enable them to observe the work of the main courses, and to study questions appropriate to their rank and responsibilities.

" The year reviewed by this report was again notable for the great difficulties experienced by many police authorities in maintaining the numbers necessary to efficiency. The improvement in conditions of service intended by the reduction in the hours of duty from 48 to 44 a week meant, in most cases, a temporary improvement in the weekly pay packet by way of payment for extra hours worked, instead of great opportunities for leisure. In this way the cost of the police to the community has increased, without the real object of the reform having been achieved. For the first year since the war the numbers appointed on probation did not reach anything like the numbers who left the several forces, so that the year ended with fewer police on duty than when it began. This is a serious problem, to the solution of which close study should be given by the responsible authorities."

GLOSSARY

For the benefit of students of Criminology, it may be of interest to record terms and phrases which are in common use among the police forces and, even more current, among members of the criminal classes.

Rhyming slang is omitted. It enjoyed a considerable vogue but is now perhaps more popular with Cockney comedians on the music-halls than in the underworld.

The following list is not exhaustive. It will be appreciated that, for obvious reasons, criminals show a tendency to vary their jargon from time to time.

Broadsman	Cardsharper
Busy	Detective
Casing a joint	Preliminary inspection by burglars
Claim	Arrest
Dabs	Fingerprints
Fan	Search
Fence	Receiver
Grass	Inform
Heavy Mob	Flying Squad
Hoister	Shoplifter
Kettle	Watch
Kite	Cheque
Lawing	Posing as police officers
Manor	Police district
Mr. Wood	Truncheon
Nick	Arrest
Peter	Safe
Pinch	Arrest
Porridge	Prison
Pussies	Furs
Reefer	Marihuana

Screw	Warder
Smoke	London
Snide	Counterfeit
Snout	Informer (also, prison slang for tobacco)
Snow	Cocaine
Spieler	Gaming house
Spike	Workhouse
Squeeze	Silk
Stool	Informer
Sweeny Todd	Flying Squad
Tail	Shadow
Tearaway	Ruffian
Whizzers	Pickpockets